A Queen of the past is not an Ex-Queen.
~ JOHN RUSKIN

Women have been called queens for a long time,
but the kingdom given them isn't worth ruling.
~ LOUISA MAY ALCOTT

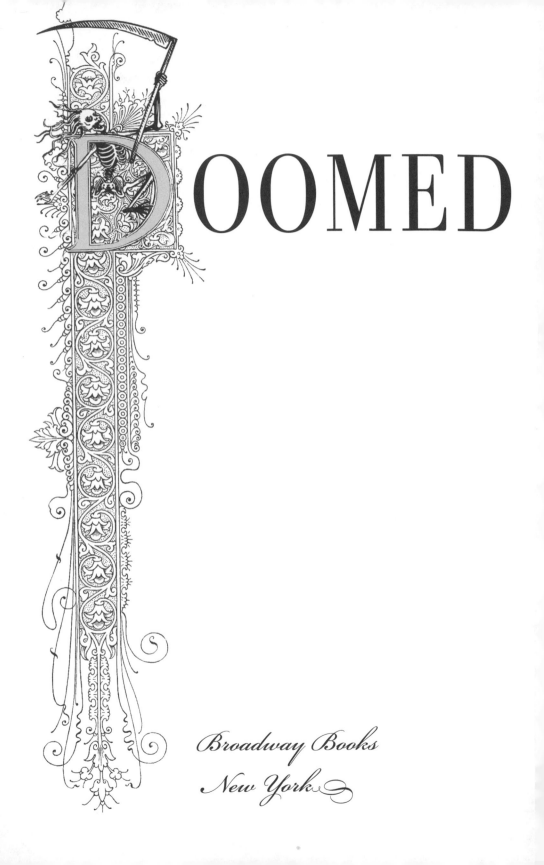

DOOMED

Broadway Books

New York

QUEENS

Kris Waldherr

*For Theresa Park, a queen among women—
with affection and appreciation*

PUBLISHED BY BROADWAY BOOKS

Copyright © 2008 by Kris Waldherr

All Rights Reserved

Published in the United States by Broadway Books,
an imprint of The Doubleday Publishing Group,
a division of Random House, Inc., New York.
www.broadwaybooks.com

BROADWAY BOOKS and its logo,
a letter B bisected on the diagonal,
are trademarks of Random House, Inc.

Book design by Kris Waldherr

Library of Congress Cataloging-in-Publication Data

Waldherr, Kris.
Doomed queens / Kris Waldherr. -- 1st ed.
  p. cm.
1. Queens--Biography. 2. Empresses--Biography. I. Title.
D107.3.W35 2008
920.72--dc22

2008021959

ISBN 978-0-7679-2899-1

PRINTED IN THE UNITED STATES OF AMERICA

3 5 7 9 10 8 6 4 2

First Edition

Contents

☠

INTRODUCTION

[The executioner] shall not have much trouble, for I have a little neck.
I shall be known as *la reine sans tête*.

~ANNE BOLEYN

elcome to your favorite dream—and worst nightmare. You are cosseted in silk, crowned with gold, and bowed to. Courtiers laugh at your jokes and compliment your beauty, even when you know you're having a bad hair day. All envy you, but things change. Just years later, even those who admired you steer clear of your path. Your influence is on the wane for any number of reasons. The fault could be yours—maybe you weren't as clever as you thought in the scheming department. Or it could be that others are scheming against you.

When the end finally comes, it arrives with the stroke of an ax at noon—a topsy-turvy Cinderella tale—or with a drumrolled march to the scaffold. The battlefield may provide you with a convenient grave. Or you might lose your crown as you labor to bring forth an heir to the kingdom. Biology becomes destiny. Best case scenario: You will survive a coup and be allowed to live out your days in awkward exile, where opportunistic stragglers will still suck up to your royal majesty, just in case.

No matter how your end finally arrives, one truth remains: Your fall from grace is not your call, though your actions may encourage it. It is your fate. After all, you are a doomed queen—and, if one is to go by the lessons of history, the only good queen is a dead one.

For too many royal women throughout history, the scenario I've sketched here was their dark reality. The members of the doomed queens club—a club I suspect few would care to join—are legion, stretching from biblical times to the present day. Their names range from the infamous—Cleopatra, Anne Boleyn, Marie Antoinette—to those whose deaths are hidden within footnotes, such as Blanche of Bourbon and Thessalonike.

Within *Doomed Queens* I've presented fifty of these lives from around the globe and throughout the ages. While each queen's final destiny may differ, one fact remains consistent: Despite the perks of royalty, it's usually not good to be the queen.

What was it about being royal that made so many women so vulnerable to losing their lives for power? Let me count the ways—here is an admittedly abbreviated overview of the doomed queen:

BED, BIBLICAL TIMES, AND BEYOND: It has always been obvious that the female of the species holds the keys to the kingdom—the kingdom of life, that is. Without the fruit of the womb, humanity would crash and burn. Boo-hoo, what's a power-loving man to do? To solve this problem, mating and relating is safely confined within the institution of matrimony and becomes sanctified with religious rites. The power of female fertility is harnessed, thus creating dynastic succession. Royal women who get uppity with the system get offed. Watch out, Olympias and Cleopatra!

YO, LET'S GET CIVILIZED: Power isn't enough—there's money, too. The Dark Ages roll in, disquieting queens everywhere. Men try their darnedest to hold on to property beyond the grave, despite that whole can't-take-it-with-you dilemma. Salic law, which sprang from the Frankish empire, becomes institutionalized. An excerpt: *The whole inheritance of the land shall come to the male sex.* But if women can't inherit property, can they inherit thrones? Over time, Salic law leads to lots of territorial fighting when a male heir isn't available.

MARRIAGE MAKES THE WORLD GO 'ROUND: No male heir? No problem! To avoid war, the powers that be send their daughters to sleep with their enemies and bear their children, keeping it all in the family. But are these queens royal consorts or royal hostages? The Austrian Hapsburg dynasty, whose rise to power peaks during the Renaissance, is especially adept at this clever little maneuver. Their family motto? "Leave others to make war, while you, lucky Austria, marry." Like chess queens, women are moved about the game board but are sacrificed first to protect the king—especially if their wombs prove infertile or if they become too power hungry.

POWER TO THE PEOPLE: With the start of the Age of Enlightenment, blue bloods shake in their boots. Power has shifted to the people, as embodied by the press, who no longer respects the sanctity of royalty. *Vive la révolution*—or not, if your name happens to be Marie Antoinette. Later in history, the media can make or break a reign, as in the cases of Caroline of Brunswick, a nineteenth-century queen of England, and Diana Spencer, a twentieth-century queen of hearts.

And now we have reached the twenty-first century. Are there still doomed queens among us? Certainly! Though we have moved on from the guillotine (which was last used by the French government in 1977), the doomed queen still lives and dies. These days, she might not be as easily recognizable as she once was. She may not have royal blood either. Tiaras are de rigueur for red carpets, but today's doomed queen is more likely to be attired in business best or haute couture. She could be part of a political dynasty, wield the wealth of a global corporation, or bear overwhelming celebrity.

Recognize her now? Just in case, here are two more examples ripped from news headlines. At the time of this writing, Benazir Bhutto, the first woman ruler of an Islamic nation, was assassinated after returning to Pakistan to reclaim the power she once wielded. Meanwhile, rumors fly that Pakistan's current president or his supporters could be responsible for her death. In the United States, former first lady Hillary Clinton has lost the democratic nomination for the presidency. Did first mate Bill muscle her into oblivion on the campaign trail?

DOOMED KINGS?

or Why Ladies Only

The sad reality is that the threat level leaps from ecru to red when the head wearing the crown is missing a Y chromosome. Why are male rulers less doomed?

While kings were also vulnerable to political upheaval—just ask Louis XVI, Marie Antoinette's headless husband—for the most part men pulled the strings at court. Therefore any woman blocking the way to power was a threat to be eliminated. Common ways to bump off an inconvenient consort included beheading, burning, drowning, poison, stabbing, strangling, starving, and forcing suicide.

The justifications for their deaths were usually based on underlying issues such as religious differences, infertility, or dynastic struggles. And when there wasn't an easy way to dump a queen, the men got creative. For example, in order to gain the right to slice off Anne Boleyn's comely head, Henry VIII accused her of treason with a side of adultery.

Women were also more vulnerable to the travails of the flesh. While they usually didn't go to war, potential royal brood mares were often sent on treacherous journeys to wed. After marriage, childbirth was a dangerous rite of passage many did not survive.

Whatever your opinion of Clinton or Bhutto, there's one point we can all agree on: Their femaleness was—and is—considered a liability in their quest for power.

Like it or not, it's still a man's world. As such, the doomed queen reflects our uneasiness with women of power, even in these advanced times. The not-so-subliminal message at hand is that women who strive upward do so at their own risk.

In closing, I leave you with a story that originated in Vienna, land of the marriage-happy Hapsburgs. In olden times, a masked ball was held to which all of society was invited. During the ball, a queen danced with a handsome gentleman, whose identity was concealed by a red mask. As the night wore on, she fell madly in love with him, not realizing that he was the executioner on a break—royalty and death waltzing together in an intimate *danse macabre*. So it has been since the first crown was donned.

Before we commence our *danse macabre* through queenly history, here are a few notes to help you enjoy the ride.

The queens' stories are arranged chronologically according to date of demise or dethronement; when the exact year is uncertain, I've used the last date they were noted within history's annals. During my research, when confronted with contradictory information, I've striven to present that which appeared most historically persuasive. However, when all things were equal, I allowed the scales to tip toward the more colorful version.

The art and graphics presented within *Doomed Queens* are adapted from numerous sources. The full-page portraits are my original drawings, some of which were inspired by famous paintings. Many of the other decorative elements were adapted from Victorian-era ornaments or portraits of historical personages.

While some of these doomed queens' lives are certainly tragic, others are so over the top that they invite disbelief or humor. Whether you find yourself laughing or crying, I hope you will consider their examples cautionary tales for modern women who yearn to avoid the sharp edge of the sword. Humor aside, what's revealed here is serious stuff: the shadow side of feminine power in all its unsavory glory.

May you read and beware.

GRAPHICS KEY

 assassinated or cause of death unknown

 died of illness

 beheaded

 imprisoned

 burned to death

 poisoned

 death by paparazzi

 sent to religious orders

 deposed

 stabbed

 died in childbirth

 strangled

 divorced/annulled

 starved to death

 drowned

committed suicide

THE DOOMED QUEEN IN HISTORY
a time line

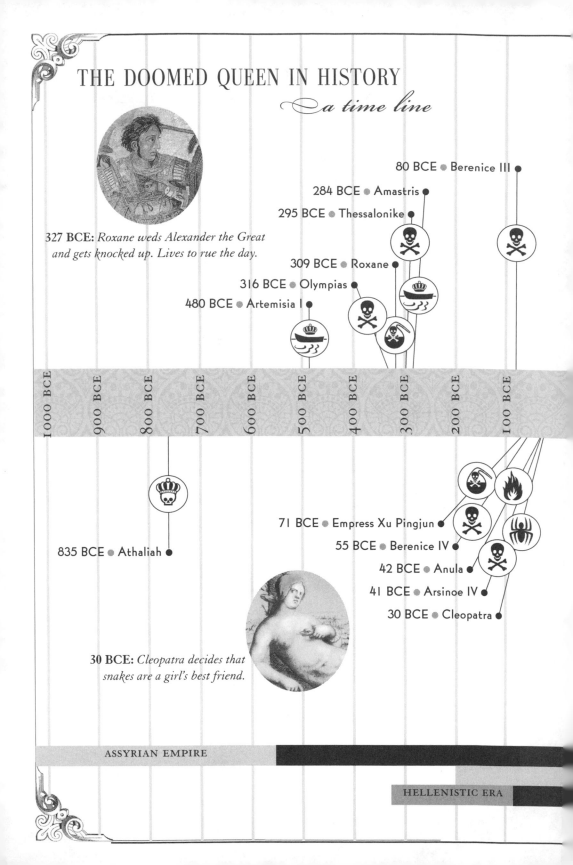

327 BCE: *Roxane weds Alexander the Great and gets knocked up. Lives to rue the day.*

80 BCE ● Berenice III ●

284 BCE ● Amastris ●

295 BCE ● Thessalonike ●

309 BCE ● Roxane ●

316 BCE ● Olympias ●

480 BCE ● Artemisia I ●

1000 BCE | 900 BCE | 800 BCE | 700 BCE | 600 BCE | 500 BCE | 400 BCE | 300 BCE | 200 BCE | 100 BCE

835 BCE ● Athaliah ●

71 BCE ● Empress Xu Pingjun ●

55 BCE ● Berenice IV ●

42 BCE ● Anula ●

41 BCE ● Arsinoe IV ●

30 BCE ● Cleopatra ●

30 BCE: *Cleopatra decides that snakes are a girl's best friend.*

ASSYRIAN EMPIRE

HELLENISTIC ERA

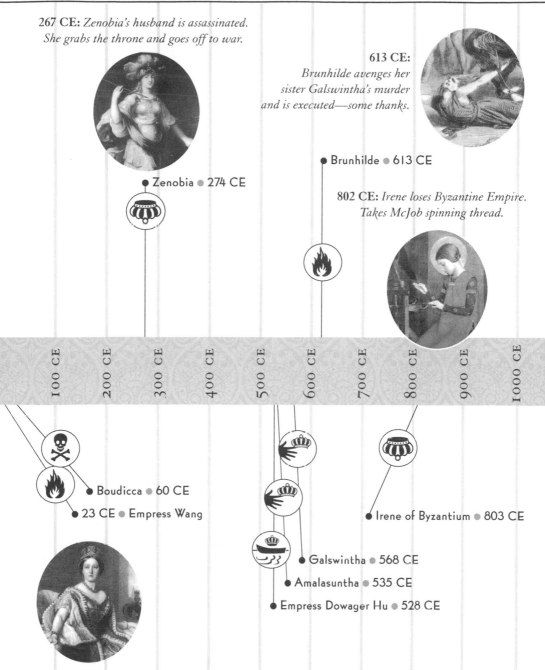

267 CE: *Zenobia's husband is assassinated. She grabs the throne and goes off to war.*

613 CE: *Brunhilde avenges her sister Galswintha's murder and is executed—some thanks.*

Brunhilde ● 613 CE

802 CE: *Irene loses Byzantine Empire. Takes McJob spinning thread.*

Zenobia ● 274 CE

100 CE 200 CE 300 CE 400 CE 500 CE 600 CE 700 CE 800 CE 900 CE 1000 CE

● Boudicca ● 60 CE

23 CE ● Empress Wang

Irene of Byzantium ● 803 CE

● Galswintha ● 568 CE

● Amalasuntha ● 535 CE

● Empress Dowager Hu ● 528 CE

60 CE: *Boudicca rules Britannia but dies in battle. Inspires Queen Victoria to rule Britannia but send others to battle.*

PERSIAN EMPIRE

HAN DYNASTY

BYZANTINE EMPIRE

ROMAN EMPIRE

MIDDLE AGES

HOLY ROMAN EMPIRE

1095: *Crusades begin with intent to popularize Christianity. Result is death and destruction. Queen Sibyl joins the fun; dies in an epidemic in 1190 while camping out with her two daughters.*

1285 ● Theodora of Trebizond ●

1248 ● Oghul Ghaimish ●

1213 ● Gertrude of Meran ●

1284:
Theodora finds religion and saves butt.

1100 CE 1200 CE 1300 CE 1400 CE 1500 CE

1361 ● Blanche of Bourbon ●

1382 ● Joan I of Naples ●

1395 ● Maria of Hungary ●

1126 ● Urraca of Castile ●

1190 ● Sibyl of Jerusalem ●

1536 ● Catherine of Aragon ●

1536 ● Anne Boleyn ●

1537 ● Jane Seymour ●

1542 ● Catherine Howard ●

1533: *Divorce, English style: Catherine of Aragon is tossed aside by Henry VIII for a new church.*

BYZANTINE EMPIRE

MIDDLE AGES

THE RENAISSANCE

HOLY ROMAN EMPIRE

MONGOL EMPIRE

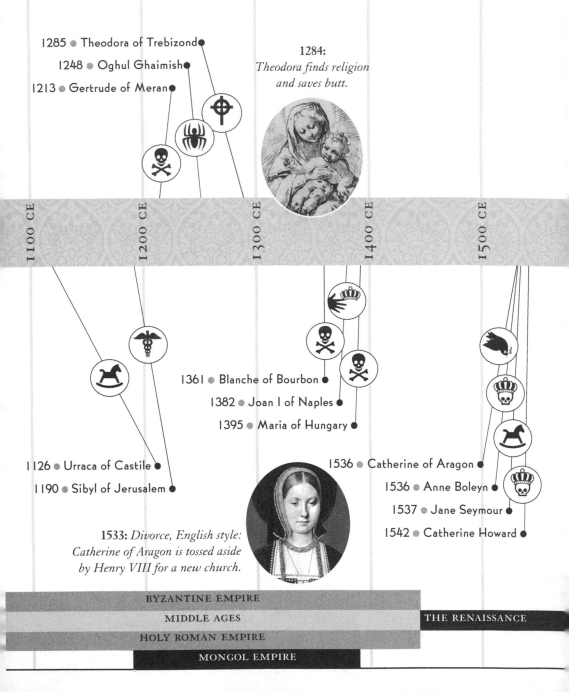

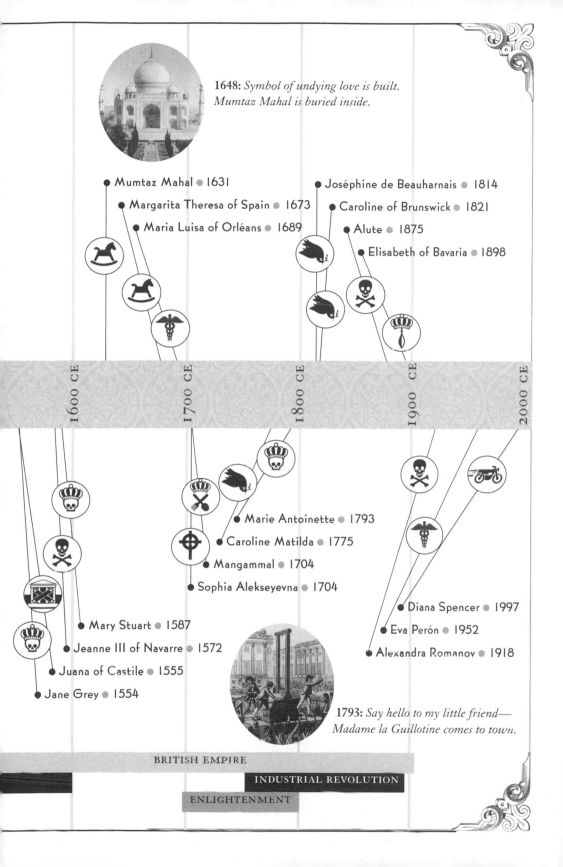

1648: *Symbol of undying love is built. Mumtaz Mahal is buried inside.*

Mumtaz Mahal ● 1631

Margarita Theresa of Spain ● 1673

Maria Luisa of Orléans ● 1689

Joséphine de Beauharnais ● 1814

Caroline of Brunswick ● 1821

Alute ● 1875

Elisabeth of Bavaria ● 1898

1600 CE   1700 CE   1800 CE   1900 CE   2000 CE

Marie Antoinette ● 1793

Caroline Matilda ● 1775

Mangammal ● 1704

Sophia Alekseyevna ● 1704

Diana Spencer ● 1997

Eva Perón ● 1952

Alexandra Romanov ● 1918

Mary Stuart ● 1587

Jeanne III of Navarre ● 1572

Juana of Castile ● 1555

Jane Grey ● 1554

1793: *Say hello to my little friend—*
Madame la Guillotine comes to town.

BRITISH EMPIRE

INDUSTRIAL REVOLUTION

ENLIGHTENMENT

CHAPTER ONE

Biblical Times and Beyond

OUT OF THE MOUTHS OF BABES
Mine honor was not yielded, but conquered merely.

Cleopatra,
via William Shakespeare

*I*t is in the ancient world that our survey of unfortunate queens begins. This era is anchored by two figures, Alexander the Great and Cleopatra. Though the two rulers shared little beyond a common ancestor and some serious ambition, both served to inspire the destruction of those close to them. Just call them the Typhoid Marys of blue bloods.

Alexander was a descendant of the powerful Argead dynasty that ruled the vast Macedonian empire in the fourth century BCE. He used his considerable military genius to expand his holdings to encompass just about all of the ancient world, spreading the best of Greek culture (better known as Hellenism) in the process. Alexander's premature demise in 323 BCE led to numerous power struggles and fatalities. His death also led to the founding of Egypt's Ptolemaic dynasty, from which Cleopatra sprang like Athena from Zeus's head.

The saga of Cleopatra and her kin is, in many ways, a tale of sibling rivalry gone wild. Cleopatra lived three centuries after Alexander and was the last pharaoh of the Ptolemaic dynasty. Though she was a skilled ruler, she was no warrior like her ancestor—instead, she seduced influential men into fighting her battles for her. Her two regent sisters, Berenice and Arsinoe, also coveted the Egyptian throne but weren't as persuasive in the charm department. Nor did they have Cleo's canny intelligence.

What exactly was it about Egypt that encouraged women rulers to set their caps so high? The historian Herodotus proposed that things were just different there: "The people, in most of their manners and customs, exactly reverse the common practice of mankind. For example women attend the markets and trade, while men sit at home at the loom. . . . Women urinate standing up, men sitting down. . . ."

And how did these queens of biblical times end their reigns? Matricide occurred too often for comfort—offspring hungry for power did not allow sweet memories of the womb to discourage their desires. Also popular: poison, drowning, and state-sanctioned suicides. Fun times.

Athaliah

835 BCE

mong royals of the biblical age, Queen Athaliah had quite the pedigree. She was the daughter of Israel's King Ahab and Queen Jezebel—yes, *that* Jezebel, the temptress immortalized in blues songs and an old Bette Davis movie. The Book of Kings claims that Athaliah's infamous mother met a nasty end at the hands of palace eunuchs. As for Athaliah, her life and death illustrate the adage of the apple not falling far from the tree.

Royal marriages in biblical times were no different from royal marriages later in history—dynastic aspirations have ever trumped personal inclination. Jezebel, a princess of Phoenicia, was pragmatically wed to King Ahab to ally their lands against enemies. Like mother, like daughter: When Athaliah came of age, her parents trundled the princess of Israel off to King Jehoram of Judah to say "I do." Ideally speaking, their union should have created one big happy conglomerate of Judah-Israel where everyone lived in harmony. But there was one problem: Athaliah followed her mother's worship of Baal, a Mesopotamian fertility god; Jehoram was a descendant of King David. Today, these differences would make prime ingredients for a screwball comedy where everyone learns religious tolerance and how to make a mean matzo ball. In ancient times, they usually spelled bloodshed.

When Athaliah married Jehoram, Jehoram agreed to take on Athaliah's religion. The new queen of Judah gave birth to a son named Ahaziah, who also followed his mother's lead in worship.

Though they all may have gotten along in private, in public Jehoram's rule was unstable—his subjects weren't too happy with the king's religion by marriage. Nor did they limit themselves to complaints. Jehoram was

A BRIEF DIGRESSION

Executions were performed during ancient times for a wide range of infractions beyond murder or treason. The Code of Hammurabi, the first set of written laws, which dates from 1760 BCE Mesopotamia, lists numerous death-worthy offenses, such as bearing false witness or hiding runaway slaves. Methods to dispatch the condemned to the next world included, in no particular order: starvation, hanging, poison, decapitation, strangulation, crucifixion, and stoning. Slaves were deemed unworthy of any official ceremony and simply beaten to death.

But what about royal women like Athaliah? The Bible states that "they slew Athaliah with the sword"; one assumes this means a beheading rather than a picturesque fencing match. However, this fate was not shared by all condemned queens. Jezebel, Athaliah's mother, was killed by defenestration—a fancy way of saying she was shoved out a window. Her body was left where it landed and devoured by dogs.

fatally shot with an arrow after defending his mother-in-law from accusations of witchcraft and fornication. Ahaziah succeeded his father as king but died a year later in battle.

Now it was Athaliah's chance to rule, for bad and worse. Grabbing the opportunity presented by her son's death, she immediately ordered the executions of all possible successors to the throne of Judah—in other words, every member of her family by marriage. However, Queen Athaliah wasn't as thorough in her machinations as she thought. Her sister-in-law Jehosheba escaped the communal bloodbath, taking the queen's baby grandson, Joash, with her. She hid him and his nurse in a bedroom, a simple but evidently effective plan.

While Athaliah ruled without impediment, Jehosheba secretly raised little Joash away from the queen's attention. Six years later in 835 BCE, Joash went public and was anointed king by the powers that be.

Not surprisingly, Athaliah was furious at the royal coup. She tore at her clothes and screamed, "Treason! Treason!" But the queen's accusations were no match against King Joash's army. They captured Athaliah and promptly executed her.

CAUTIONARY MORAL
When completing a job,
don't overlook the small details.

Artemisia I

480 BCE

rtemisia became the sole regent of Halicarnassus, a city on the coast of Caria (part of modern-day Turkey), after the death of her husband in the fifth century BCE. Her husband was evidently not as intriguing as she was—his name has been lost by time. However, their union did bring forth a son, Pisindelis, who joined Artemisia in battle as an adult.

As queen, Artemisia was denounced as a tyrant because she brown-nosed King Xerxes I of Persia despite the wishes of her people. In her defense, Halicarnassus was a client city of Persia, so it was good politics to keep the big kids on the block happy.

Toward that end, Artemisia promised aid when Xerxes went to war with Greece. She also advised the king: "Do not fight at sea, for the Greeks are infinitely superior to us in naval matters." He ignored her warning and lost the water-based Battle of Salamis in 480 BCE. Artemisia participated in the battle and commanded five large ships. But when the fight turned against her, the queen attacked and sank an ally ship, thus convincing the Greeks she had defected to their side. After she escaped to safety, the Greeks were peeved at her deception and offered ten thousand drachmas for her capture.

Was Artemisia a prudent warrior seeking to limit casualties on her side? Or was she a coward trying to save her derriere? It depends on how you look at it. One rumor claimed that the queen conveniently carried two different flags into battle; she raised the Persian flag on her ship while chasing Greeks but substituted the Greek flag when they sailed too close for comfort.

Yet the historian Herodotus thought highly of Artemisia. He wrote in his *Histories*: "I must speak of a certain leader named Artemisia, whose par-

LA MÉTHODE DE MORT

Drowning

Throughout the ages, drowning was more often deployed to torture witches than to rid a nation of an unloved monarch. However, as a suicide method, drowning wields a romantic spell, all the way from heartbroken Artemisia's final plunge to Virginia Woolf's stroll with rock-filled pockets into the River Ouse. This attraction can be partly traced to a belief that drowning was a painless way to die; once the struggle for life ceased, the victim was thought to exit the world surrounded by serene visions and heavenly choirs.

No doubt this belief has roots in physical reality: When a person drowns to death, her brain becomes deprived of oxygen. And brains deprived of oxygen typically hallucinate, whether there's religion involved or not.

ticipation in the attack upon Greece, notwithstanding that she was a woman, moves my special wonder. . . . [Her] brave spirit and manly daring sent her forth to the war, when no need required her to adventure." He concluded by praising the advice she offered Xerxes. Nor does Xerxes appear to have held a grudge against her. Or maybe he did not identify her as the naval force who sunk his battleship—after all, dead sailors can't squeal. In any event, the king requested her counsel again. This time he listened and won victory.

Protected by Persia, Halicarnassus prospered under Artemisia's rule. However, one story claims that Xerxes could not protect the queen from her emotions. Later in life, Artemisia fell hard for a boy toy named Dardanus. Alas, her affections were not reciprocated. After gouging out Dardanus's eyes while he slept, Artemisia ended her reign by jumping into the sea.

CAUTIONARY MORAL
*Don't let your heart
overrule your head.*

24

Olympias

316 BCE

ithout Olympias, Alexander the Great could never have existed—and without Alexander, the civilizing force of Hellenism would not have flapped its great wings over Western culture. Olympias was queen to Philip II of Macedon; their only issue was a son who grew up to be known as Alexander the Great. For this, one must grant Olympias thanks. History would be far less interesting without him.

The birth of Alexander the Great was one of Olympias's few contributions to society. Beyond this, she was known for her affection for snakes and violence. The queen was never one to avoid dispatching a rival, real or imagined, to the great beyond. She approached murder with a ghoulish creativity that appalled even her devoted son, who loved her beyond all others except for one other person—but that's Roxane's story, still to come.

When Olympias met Philip, Philip was yet another Greek warrior king accustomed to marrying his enemies' daughters to ensure peace; a joke from that time claimed that he took on a new wife after each battle campaign. Olympias was wife number four. On top of this, Philip also enjoyed the company of men as more than friends.

After three docile war brides, Olympias was a walk on the wild side. An orphaned princess hailing from Epirus, Olympias's first loyalty was to the god Dionysus and his ecstatic mysteries, which involved dancing, snake handling, and much alcohol consumption. Plutarch writes that she "was wont in the dances proper to these ceremonies to have great tame serpents about her, which . . . made a spectacle which men could not look upon without terror." Amazingly enough, the Macedonian king fell in love with Olympias while participating in these rituals.

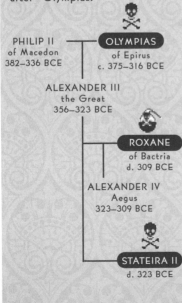

THE HOUSE OF
ARGEAD

or

*When Empire Building
Is a Bad Thing*

Olympias was the daughter of Neoptolemus, the king of the Molossians; the Molossians were a tribe in Epirus, a region located in what is now northwest Greece. Though Philip had other wives, none could compare to—or survive after—Olympias.

PHILIP II
of Macedon
382–336 BCE

OLYMPIAS
of Epirus
c. 375–316 BCE

ALEXANDER III
the Great
356–323 BCE

ROXANE
of Bactria
d. 309 BCE

ALEXANDER IV
Aegus
323–309 BCE

STATEIRA II
d. 323 BCE

Their marriage was filled with portents from the start. The night before the wedding, Olympias dreamed that a thunderbolt fell upon her body and kindled a great fire that spread over the land before it was extinguished. Soon after, Philip dreamed that he sealed her genitals with a wax seal imprinted with a lion's image. A wise man assured the king that this vision meant that the queen was pregnant with a boy as courageous as a lion.

Divine omens or no, it was clear from the start that Alexander was meant for great things. To place him on the fast track for world domination, Olympias went far beyond what even the most devoted Texas cheerleader mom would consider. Philip grew uncomfortable with her zeal and cut off marital relations after he found her sleeping next to a serpent. He decided that the queen was either an enchantress or making whoopie with the god Zeus, who often took on animal forms to seduce mortal women.

In either case, Philip felt threatened. To protect himself, the king chose to dump Olympias as queen, disinherit Alexander, and take yet another wife, Cleopatra Eurydice, who was of pure Macedonian blood. The results were incendiary. Olympias insinuated that Alexander was indeed the son of Zeus and the divine superior of Philip. Soon Philip was stabbed to death by a jealous male lover. Not surprisingly, Olympias's fingerprints were all over the plot. One rumor claimed that she plied the murderer with words to inflame his anger. She even placed a gold crown upon the executed murderer's corpse—hardly the act of a mourning widow. To ensure Alexander's reign would be unimpeded, Olympias assassinated Cleopatra Eurydice and her two small children by Philip. In a scenario out of a Grimms' fairy tale, the children were roasted to death, their mother forced to hang herself.

From here, there was no stopping Alexander—or Olympias. After he took off to conquer the world, she never saw him again. Nonetheless, she wrote him frequently. He bore her advice patiently, though he rarely took it. In turn she, too, did as she wished. When Antipater, his governor in Macedon, wrote Alexander to complain about Olympias's meddling, Alexander remarked, "Antipater does not realize that one tear of a mother erases ten thousand letters like this."

As predicted, Alexander was as brave as a lion—but even lions are vulnerable. After conquering much of the world, Alexander died in 323 BCE from a suspiciously sudden illness. He was only thirty-three.

Without Alexander's protection, Olympias knew her days were numbered. She returned to Epirus to plot her return to power but met her match in Antipater's son Cassander, who inherited Alexander's throne. He arranged for the queen's execution in 316 BCE. As a final insult, he denied her the rites of burial.

CAUTIONARY MORAL

Religion can take you only so far.

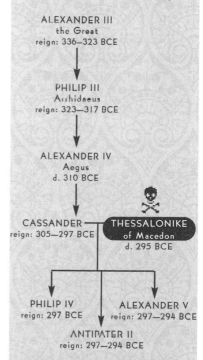

Alexander did not name an heir to his empire. When asked on his deathbed, he cryptically replied, "To the strongest." Chaos ensued. Alexander's wife Roxane gave birth to a son after his death, whom she named after his father. In the meantime, the throne was kept warm for Alex Junior by Alex Senior's older half brother Philip, who was mentally impaired; many believed Olympias had poisoned him for fun and profit. The empire became mired in civil war, aided and abetted by Olympias's scheming.

ALEXANDER III
the Great
reign: 336–323 BCE

↓

PHILIP III
Arrhidaeus
reign: 323–317 BCE

↓

ALEXANDER IV
Aegus
d. 310 BCE

↓

CASSANDER — THESSALONIKE
reign: 305–297 BCE | of Macedon
d. 295 BCE

PHILIP IV   ALEXANDER V
reign: 297 BCE   reign: 297–294 BCE
ANTIPATER II
reign: 297–294 BCE

After much strife, an eventual victor emerged in the form of Cassander, the son of Alexander's most trusted deputy Antipater. He married Alexander's half sister, Thessalonike, thus continuing Alexander's bloodline.

Roxane

309 BCE

ne has to feel compassion for Roxane, queen to Alexander the Great. Though her beauty made her the toast of the ancient world, she simply couldn't compete with Alexander's number one love. Surprisingly, this all-encompassing passion wasn't his mother, Olympias (though the king certainly loved her best of all women). Nor was it world domination (though he slept with a copy of Homer's *Iliad* by his side). Nope, it was a man, Hephaestion. And when Hephaestion died, Roxane's life went to hell in a handbasket.

Hephaestion was Alexander's favorite childhood friend. When they came of age, evidence suggests that their friendship became a friendship with benefits. Olympias did everything she could to discourage their intense attachment. She even sent her son a famed courtesan, to ease him into heterosexuality. But Alexander refused to do the deed with her—the courtesan could not compare to his beloved Hephaestion.

Had Alexander not conquered Persia, Roxane would probably have been married off to some minor warlord, hopefully to live and die in peaceful obscurity. Instead, she became enmeshed in a dynastic struggle that brought the lives of herself and her son to premature ends.

Roxane was the daughter of Oxyartes, king of Bactria, a region in what is now Afghanistan. Her name translates as "Little Star," presumably in reference to her luminous beauty. The royalty of Bactria used the fortress of Sogdian Rock as a refuge when threatened; Sogdian Rock was surrounded by a sheer cliff no one could surmount—until Alexander. In 327 BCE Alexander sent three hundred of his best climbers

Coin of the realm featuring the emperor himself.

to scale the cliff in the middle of the night. Come morning, they greeted Oxyartes and company with pancakes and mimosas. The Bactrian king was so unnerved by Alexander's success that he surrendered without a fight. He also surrendered Roxane's hand to Alexander. Hephaestion served as best man.

Though Plutarch claimed that it was love at first sight, this seems unlikely: Alexander had eyes only for Hephaestion. Marrying Roxane was a savvy political move to solidify alliances. To his credit, Alexander wed Roxane using the ceremonies of her people, which won him much respect— he didn't just invade, he assimilated. It was for similar reasons that three years later Alexander married Stateira, the daughter of the Persian king Darius III, after he conquered that land. Their union was part of a mass Moonie-style wedding that Alexander insisted his soldiers partake in— the ultimate consolidation of power.

Roxane's life with Alexander was one long military slog. Legend claims that she traveled with him to India, which was feared as an exotic realm no one could conquer. Alexander could not resist the challenge but emerged unvictorious. However, even the toughest campaign was a cinch compared to the queen's life after Hephaestion's unexpected death in 324 BCE. Alexander was never the same. He died several months later, also of a sudden illness—some believe he and Hephaestion were poisoned—but not before knocking up Roxane a mere six years after their wedding.

Fate might have been kinder had Roxane given birth to a girl—but she didn't. It is surprising that Roxane and Alexander Junior survived as long as they did, given the chaos after Alexander Senior's demise. To save their skins, Roxane behaved accordingly. She arranged for the murder of Alexander's other wife, Stateira. She also gained the protection of Olympias from Cassander, the warrior most likely to succeed in Alexander's empire. But this was not enough to save their lives, especially after Olympias was sent to her eternal reward.

Roxane and her twelve-year-old son were poisoned by Cassander in 309 BCE, thus marking the end of Alexander's bloodline.

CAUTIONARY MORAL
Don't marry a man in love with another man.

Thessalonike

295 BCE

fter the demise of Alexander the Great in 323 BCE, most of his surviving relatives lost their lives as they scrambled after the crumbs of his empire. One notable exception was Alexander's half sister Thessalonike.

How did Thessalonike escape being served death on a platter when so many others could not? Perhaps it was because she hardly knew Alexander—Thessalonike was only a small child when her big brother took off to conquer the world. It could also be because she was the daughter of Philip II's mistress Nicesipolis. Nicesipolis died soon after Thessalonike's birth in 342 BCE, leaving the girl to be raised by Olympias. As incredible as it sounds, Alexander's mother felt affection for Thessalonike and taught her the ways of Dionysus. At the very least, Olympias did not judge the girl an impediment to her worldly ambitions.

However, though Thessalonike made it past the first round of eliminations, she did not survive the second.

Upon Alexander's death, Thessalonike took refuge with her stepmother, Olympias, against Cassander, who grabbed Alexander's throne. Several years later, Cassander finally had the cojones to dispatch Olympias, but he granted a different fate to Thessalonike: He married her. Their union in 315 BCE gave the new king's reign a legitimacy it previously lacked.

After going through so much, you would think that Thessalonike had it made. From an illegitimate birth, she had climbed the ladder of royal success to become queen of it all. Presumably the couple got along well enough, since three sons—Philip, Antipater, and Alexander—soon arrived. Cassander even named a city after Thessalonike, granting her great honor. But these ties of blood and bed were unable to prevent the queen from participating in a Macedonian version of *King Lear*.

When it comes to ruling a kingdom, three sons are two too many. After Cassander succumbed to dropsy in 297 BCE, Thessalonike used the teachings of her wily stepmother to manipulate Philip, Antipater, and Alexander to her advantage. But the queen was no Olympias—death soon visited them all.

Philip, the eldest son, wasted away from a mysterious illness not long after taking charge. Two years later, middle son, Antipater, became jealous of Thessalonike's attentions to Alexander and murdered his mother in 295 BCE. Not one to be left out of a family squabble, Alexander bumped off Antipater but was then assassinated himself by a pretender to the throne.

Though Thessalonike's mortal remains are long gone, she is remembered within the annals of Greek folklore. One legend claims that upon her death, the queen was transformed into a mermaid who lives still in the Aegean Sea.

CAUTIONARY MORAL
When it comes to succession,
one heir is plenty.

A BRIEF DIGRESSION
Stories about mermaids date from about 1000 BCE, some 700 years before Thessalonike. Even then, mermaids were associated with disappointing relationships. The first known mermaid legend tells of the ancient Assyrian goddess Atargatis, who drowned herself after a disastrous love affair. Though she hoped to be transformed into a fish, her divine nature would not cooperate—she retained her human form above the waist.

Amastris

284 BCE

The deaths of Thessalonike and her family brought the annihilation of the descendants of Alexander the Great to a close. However, aftershocks from his legacy rocked the ancient world for some years. One victim they eventually claimed was Amastris, the queen of Heraclea Pontica, a Greek colony on the coast of what is now Turkey.

Amastris was the daughter of Oxyathres, the brother of the Persian king Darius III. Remember that mass wedding staged by Alexander to commemorate grabbing Persia from King Darius? Amastris was one of the reluctant war brides; she was married to Craterus, Alexander's favorite bachelor general. As it turned out, Craterus was just the start of the princess's complicated matrimonial career. She would have two more opportunities to register for royal china before breathing her last.

One year later in 323 BCE, Amastris's Alexander-inspired nuptials were history. When the big guy bit the dust, Craterus abandoned the princess to return to the sweetheart he'd left behind in Macedon. Before he departed, he gave his blessing to Amastris's next groom, Dionysius, the tyrant ruler of Heraclea Pontica.

Rumor held that Dionysius was so overjoyed by the death of Alex-

A BRIEF DIGRESSION

Modern dictionaries define a tyrant as a ruler who wields power through cruel or oppressive means. However, in ancient Greece a tyrant was someone who had seized the right to rule. While their reigns weren't sanctioned by law or birthright, they usually won popular support from local businesses and workers—think corporate takeover rather than military coup. The truth was that the tyrant Dionysius was loved by his subjects—they even gave him the nickname of "the Good."

ander that he abandoned himself to endless luxury and gluttony. With Alexander gone, life at the tyrant's court was a nonstop banquet, much of which was funded by Amastris, who had brought a considerable dowry. But too much of a good thing is too much: Dionysius grew morbidly obese. Nonetheless, his heft did not prevent him from gifting his consort with three children—Clearchus, Oxyathres, and a daughter named after herself—over a short period of time. Dionysius died by choking on his own fat in 306 BCE, leaving his queen to rule in trust for their sons.

Amastris resigned herself to single life. But like Penelope without Odysseus, it wasn't long before suitors clamored for the empty place on her throne and in her bed. This time, the lucky winner was Lysimachus, the latest king of Macedon. Though he loved Amastris's bountiful assets, he also loved the queen for herself. Nevertheless, Lysimachus went out for a pack of cigarettes permanently when the more politically advantageous queen of Egypt offered him her hand in marriage.

Now alone, Amastris hung up her veil for good—she chose to govern Heraclea Pontica on her own. According to the historian Memnon, the queen ruled prudently and built up the colony's strength and size. In time, she expanded her territories to found the city of Amastris. When her children entered adulthood, Amastris prepared to hand over her well-tended crown and enjoy the quiet comforts of middle age. But this was not to be.

Amastris's sons grew up to be ruthless despots, unlike their much-admired parents. The princes arranged for Amastris to be drowned when onboard a ship, perhaps to short-circuit the populace's growing dissatisfaction with their rule. The murder was quickly avenged by Lysimachus, the queen's final husband, who decided that his affection for Amastris remained as strong as his desire to regain her lands.

CAUTIONARY MORAL
Avoid boats rowed by your enemies.

Berenice III

80 BCE

erenice III was the first queen of Egypt to rule without a consort in over a millennium. Though her reign was brief, her example inspired her descendant Cleopatra to also rule alone. Improbably, neither queen possessed Egyptian blood. Berenice did not even speak Egyptian; she considered Greek her lingua franca.

How did a non-Egyptian woman ascend to the Egyptian throne? Berenice's rise to power can be traced back some two centuries earlier to Alexander the Great. When Alexander's body proved weaker than his will, his vast empire eventually suffered the fate of all empires without a strong ruler: It was cut up slice by slice by those hungry for a piece of the pie. Berenice III's ancestor Ptolemy was a distant relative of Alexander and one of his most gifted generals. Like everyone else, Ptolemy wanted in—but he was wiser than the others. Instead of overreaching for the world, he limited himself to Egypt.

Geographic isolation plus agricultural wealth equals one happy ruler. Egypt was surrounded by sea and mountains, making it unappealing for spur-of-the-moment invasions; its wealth was derived from the Nile, whose annual flooding ensured abundant harvests that the ancient world depended upon for survival. To cap his coup, Ptolemy managed to steal Alexander's corpse, which he interred in a magnificent tomb in the heart of Alexandria, Egypt's capital city. By owning the literal embodiment of Alexander, Ptolemy's reign gained an aura of legitimacy that allowed his descendants to rule Egypt for three centuries. The only power to get in their way was the Roman Empire, which they mollified with regular tributes of money.

Though Ptolemy originally hailed from Macedon, his family quickly assumed the customs of their adopted land, though not its language. Chief among them was the use of intermarriage to consolidate power. Egyptian mythology encouraged the wedding of brother to sister, niece to uncle; Ptolemy saw no reason to break with tradition. The Ptolemaic dynasty also recycled names ad nauseam, which makes it confusing to ascertain exactly who ruled when and how.

Ptolemy monotonously followed after Ptolemy for generations. Then along came Berenice, the third of her name.

Queen Berenice III was the daughter of Ptolemy IX. Her father married her off to his younger brother who, not surprisingly, was named Ptolemy X. It was uncertain whether the marriage was consummated, but it mattered not—Berenice was widowed before an heir could be born.

After her father died in 62 BCE, Berenice decided to rule without a consort at her side—one dead husband was enough. But the powers that be in Rome weren't too happy about this. To assuage them, Berenice deigned to marry her father's stepson, Ptolemy XI. Having gained Egypt by possessing the queen, Ptolemy had no further use for Berenice. He waited a scant three weeks before arranging for her murder.

This Ptolemy's reign was short. Though Berenice's reign had lasted only half a year, she won the hearts of her populace during this period. They proved their loyalty by lynching Ptolemy several days later.

CAUTIONARY MORAL
If you share your power,
you may soon lose it.

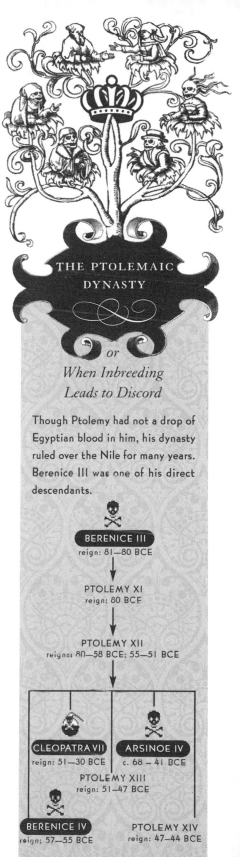

THE PTOLEMAIC
DYNASTY

or
When Inbreeding
Leads to Discord

Though Ptolemy had not a drop of Egyptian blood in him, his dynasty ruled over the Nile for many years. Berenice III was one of his direct descendants.

BERENICE III
reign: 81—80 BCE

PTOLEMY XI
reign: 80 BCE

PTOLEMY XII
reigns: 80—58 BCE; 55—51 BCE

CLEOPATRA VII
reign: 51—30 BCE

ARSINOE IV
c. 68—41 BCE

PTOLEMY XIII
reign: 51—47 BCE

BERENICE IV
reign: 57—55 BCE

PTOLEMY XIV
reign: 47—44 BCE

Empress Xu Pingjun

71 BCE

bout nine years after Queen Berenice's death in Egypt, halfway around the world another royal woman met an unnatural end. The Chinese empress Xu Pingjun lost her life to fulfill a family's quest for power. Unlike the immediately avenged Berenice, it took half a decade for Xu's assassin to be brought to justice.

This most unfortunate empress reigned during the illustrious Han dynasty; the Han dynasty's many achievements include porcelain, the first dictionary, and the proliferation of Confucianism. Xu was the devoted wife of Emperor Xuan, who had been raised as a commoner but elevated to the throne at the age of eighteen in a veritable Cinderella story. Xuan's fairy godmother was Huo Guang, a mover-and-shaker statesman with enough influence to depose the previous emperor when he proved ineffective.

Initially Xu was acknowledged only as the emperor's imperial consort. Huo advised Xuan to take a second wife for his empress, suggesting his daughter for the role—her appointment would complete Huo's passive-aggressive coup. However, the emperor truly loved his wife, who had wed him when he was poor and humble. He refused to let politics trump emotion.

Xu was crowned in 74 BCE. As empress, she never forgot her roots and, like her husband, was noted for her modest ways. Everyone could have lived happily ever after were it not for Huo Guang's wife, Lady Xian. Xian did not take the emperor's rejection of her daughter lightly. Plus she was even more ambitious than her kingmaker husband—think Lady Macbeth, Han dynasty style.

Xian watched for an opportunity to impose her will. It took her three years, but her plot was exceptionally devious. When Xu was in labor with her second child, Xian bribed the empress's female physician to add wolfsbane to her medication; wolfsbane, also known as aconite, causes asphyxiation. The timing of the murder suggested that Xu perished from postnatal complications rather than cruel intentions.

Nonetheless, after Xu's death the physician was arrested for questioning. Terrified the not so good doctor would point the finger at her, Xian lost her cool and convinced her husband to drop the case. With that crisis averted, Xian was free to concentrate on the big picture again. Soon after, the emperor made her daughter empress—she just happened to be available to comfort the grieving widower.

It would appear that the evildoers were rewarded by good fortune, but murder will out. Five years later, Emperor Xuan discovered the truth behind Xu's passing and executed most of Huo's family.

CAUTIONARY MORAL
*Choose your own doctors
and pay them well.*

*Aconite, aka wolfsbane.
Pretty but deadly.*

Poison

As Madame Bovary discovered in the novel of the same name, dying from poison ain't an easy way to go. After snacking on arsenic-laden rat poison, Flaubert's favorite adultress envisioned sinking into a peaceful unending sleep. Instead, "drops of sweat oozed from her bluish face. . . . Her teeth chattered, her dilated eyes looked vaguely about her. . . . She was seized with convulsions and cried out, 'Ah, my God! It is horrible!'" Madame Bovary's death arrived too many agonizing hours later, announced by a stream of tarlike vomit from her mouth.

Because it lacks odor and flavor, arsenic is the most popular poison for the murderously minded. Arsenic affects its victim with irreversible liver and circulatory failure—a different route to the grave than Empress Xu's experience with aconite, which depresses the cardiovascular system until the victim suffocates from a lack of oxygen. Some snake venoms act similarly but by paralyzing the nervous system; other venoms destroy red blood cells, leading to internal hemorrhage. Asps were used for executions in ancient Egypt and Greece—a more public form of poisoning than the wolfsbane hidden in poor Xu's medicine.

Berenice IV

55 BCE

ack in Egypt, another Berenice soon came along. The reign of Berenice IV as queen of Egypt was almost as truncated as that of her murdered ancestress, Berenice III. Though the later queen Berenice managed to hold on to the crown about a year longer than the earlier, neither reign was anything to write home about.

By the time Berenice IV came to power in 57 BCE, it was the twilight of the Ptolemaic dynasty. Three hundred years of inbreeding had led to internal power struggles and a weakened bloodline. Berenice was the eldest of five children born to Ptolemy XII, the Egyptian pharaoh better known as Auletes, "the flute player"; this belittling nickname referred to either his chubby cheeks or his habit of waxing musical when in his cups. Ptolemy's subjects considered him weak of mind and will, especially after he imposed high taxes to meet the demands of the increasingly greedy Roman Empire.

Ptolemy was hanging on to his throne by a thread when Rome decided to annex Cyprus, an island under Egyptian rule. The Egyptians blamed Ptolemy for the loss and riots ensued. The king fled to Rome, hoping to convince them to return Cyprus and reinforce his monarchy.

With the king away, Rome asked twenty-year-old Berenice to mind the store. Berenice went one better and declared herself queen—she was glad to be rid of her father. The people of Egypt concurred and threw their full support behind her rule. Berenice's four younger siblings Cleopatra (yes, *that* Cleopatra), Ptolemy Junior, Arsinoe, and Ptolemy Redux sucked it up to save their lives. There was little else they could do.

Berenice IV's rule was distinguished by chaos and murder. Initially, she may have had a coruler confusingly named Cleopatra—it's unclear whether this Cleopatra was her stepmother or an older sister. If so, she was immediately dispatched to the next world. Next up was Berenice's cousin, Seleucus. The uneasy queen wed him to grant her rule stability, since people weren't too thrilled to see a woman alone on the throne. The honeymoon did not last long. Seleucus was murdered within a week's time.

Berenice immediately tried marriage again, this time to Archelaus of Cappadocia. While all these couplings were going on, the queen's daddy was still scheming to regain Egypt. By now, Ptolemy had moved on from Rome to Ephesus, where he enlisted the support of the Syrians.

In 55 BCE, Ptolemy came triumphantly marching home. Paternal love did not keep him from immediately executing Berenice and her followers. One story claims that Ptolemy had Berenice's head brought to him upon a platter while Cleopatra watched. It is presumed he did not serve it for dinner.

CAUTIONARY MORAL
*When minding the store, don't get caught
with your hand in the candy jar.*

LIFE AFTER DEATH

Berenice's death made little sister Cleopatra next in line to the Egyptian throne. To keep it in the family, Ptolemy Senior insisted Cleopatra tie the knot with her brother Ptolemy Junior. Ptolemy Senior reigned for another four years before he passed away at the ripe age of sixty-six. Improbably, he died of illness rather than alcoholism or at the hands of the Romans and his scheming children.

The flute player was also father of Cleopatra, who gained the throne after Berenice.

Anula

42 BCE

Sexual cannibalism is the *Liebestod* of the insect kingdom. Two prime examples of it are the praying mantis and the black widow spider; in both species, the females dispatch their partners to the next world after making sweet love to them. Among humans, sexual cannibalism is essentially nonexistent—no doubt taboos against murder help deter postcoital violence. However, these petty social codes did not stop Queen Anula of the south Indian kingdom of Sri Lanka from sleeping and killing her way to the top.

The reign of Anula reads like a Joe Esterhas screenplay. It is recorded in the *Mahavamsa*, a chronicle of Sri Lankan history written by Buddhist monks. Just like a Sharon Stone femme fatale, the queen's rise to power involved seduction and dead bodies. By the end of Anula's reign, her modus operandi had become boringly predictable. Her weapon of choice: poison. Her preferred victims: working-class men—and the more, the better.

Little is known of Anula before she married King Coranaga, who became king in a government coup in 62 BCE. The new queen lay low for twelve years until her lust for Siva, a palace guard, spurred her to action. After so many years of marriage, Coranaga trusted his wife enough to imbibe whatever she offered. He was soon pushing up daisies.

Upon the king's demise, the crown passed to another male member of royalty; Anula was dethroned and married Siva. One presumes she missed the pleasures of sex seasoned with power—this time, she waited only three years before poisoning the monarch. She replaced him with Siva, thus restoring herself to the throne.

From here, there was no stopping Queen Anula. King Siva reigned for just over a year before Anula capriciously set her cap for a carpenter. The carpenter kept the throne warm for the woodcutter who followed; both men were quickly dispatched by the queen via her favorite method. Anula also proved to be a gifted multitasker. In the midst of all this marrying and burying, she enjoyed the sexual favors of thirty-two palace guards.

After poisoning her last consort, Queen Anula decided to reign solo. This was the final straw for her populace—apparently it was okay to murder but not to rule without a male consort. Within four months, Anula was forcibly deposed. She was trapped within the palace where she had committed her murders, which was then set on fire.

CAUTIONARY MORAL
As you climb to success over the dead,
don't alienate the living.

LA MÉTHODE DE MORT

Fire

In Malory's *Le Morte d'Arthur*, Queen Guenever was found guilty of treason and condemned to be burned to death. She was stripped of her royal robes and tied to a large stake before a jeering crowd. Lucky for her, the queen was rescued by her loyal knight Launcelot just in time.

Burning at the stake was death at its most excruciatingly painful. In Europe, it was reserved for so-called witches, homosexuals, and heretics—royal blood was beside the point—and reached its zenith in medieval times. It was also a public ritual, where scores of people gathered to watch and often to protest the proceedings. A mass was performed beforehand, usually by an up-and-coming clergyman eager for notice.

If they were lucky, the condemned would expire from smoke inhalation before the flames reached them. To ensure a rapid demise, family and friends paid the executioner to allow them to add wood to the fire. Sometimes packets of gunpowder were hung around the victims' necks, instantly killing them when ignited.

The death of Anula was far less ceremonial. Her palace fire was fueled by an angry populace seeking to get rid of a murderous ruler.

Arsinoe IV

41 BCE

rsinoe IV was the younger sister of Cleopatra, the glamorous Egyptian queen known for her alliances with Julius Caesar and Mark Antony. Besides Cleopatra, Arsinoe had three siblings: two younger brothers, both named Ptolemy, and another older sister, Berenice, whom their father Ptolemy XII executed in 55 BCE after she got too cozy with his throne.

Arsinoe was cleverer than Berenice. She waited until after their father's death to make her move for the crown of Egypt. However, she was unable to outsmart Cleopatra, who eventually arranged for her baby sister's death. As evidenced throughout their rule, the members of the Ptolemaic dynasty did not draw the line at killing kin.

When he died in 51 BCE, Ptolemy XII deeded Egypt to Cleopatra and her brother-husband Ptolemy XIII. Unsatisfied, Ptolemy XIII decided to co-opt Egypt for himself, and Arsinoe gladly came along for the ride. Julius Caesar, Rome's head honcho, soon became involved in the family fray, since it was in Rome's interest to keep Egypt economically stable. One story claims that Arsinoe was suggested to Caesar as a consort; instead, the Roman warrior succumbed to the numerous charms of Cleopatra.

Sated by sex, Caesar restored Cleopatra as Egypt's sole monarch. Arsinoe was granted the booby prize of Cyprus, so she wouldn't go home empty-handed. But Arsinoe was not pleased—she plotted revolt against Cleopatra and Caesar. Those unhappy with Cleopatra found the queen of Cyprus a convenient rallying point.

By 48 BCE, Arsinoe had whipped up enough military support to grab the throne from her big sister. She trapped Caesar and Cleopatra in the

imperial palace, but not for long—Caesar's troops arrived in early 47 BCE to free the dynamic duo. They also captured Arsinoe. She was stripped of her crowns and transported to Rome, where she was paraded in chains through the streets as a prisoner of war.

Usually prisoners of war were put to death, but Caesar had pity upon Arsinoe, perhaps because she was Cleopatra's sister. He allowed her to run away to Ephesus, where she quickly settled down in the Temple of Artemis. Amazingly enough, Arsinoe had not learned her lesson and began scheming anew. She even encouraged the temple's high priest to address her as queen.

Cleopatra's revenge came five years later. Now aligned with Mark Antony, Cleopatra convinced her lover to arrange for Arsinoe's execution. Arsinoe met her death in 41 BCE within the Temple of Artemis, where she had first claimed sanctuary.

CAUTIONARY MORAL
Blood is seldom thicker than blood.

LIFE AFTER DEATH

Arsinoe's story has been overlooked in the face of her more successful older sister, Cleopatra—too often history is written by the victors. But in death, Arsinoe was buried with the queenly honors that had been denied her in life. Her remains were interred in a tomb in the Temple of Artemis, one of the seven wonders of the ancient world. Archaeologists have never been able to locate her tomb.

Engraving of Cleopatra with Mark Antony. Baby sister Arsinoe just couldn't compete.

Cleopatra

30 BCE

leopatra ruled as queen of Egypt for more than two decades—an astonishing feat for a woman born into a dysfunctional, inbred family headed by an alcoholic pharaoh. During her reign, Cleopatra became famed for her charm and unusual intelligence; the historian Dio Cassius wrote that "she captured all who listened to her." Though Greek by blood, she identified wholeheartedly with her country's heritage; of her family, she was the only member to learn Egyptian.

Cleopatra was seventeen when her father, Ptolemy XII, passed on to the next world. He chose her to corule Egypt with her ten-year-old husband-brother, Ptolemy XIII. Despite her father's wishes, the queen was soon ousted into the desert by Ptolemy Junior's supporters—so much for spousal loyalty. But years of familial scheming taught Cleopatra how to survive. She used her time in exile to amass a large army. However, Ptolemy refused to tango with her forces. There was little Cleopatra could do. As the months passed, it became harder and harder to keep her army fed and frisky.

Fortunately, Julius Caesar arrived in Alexandria just as it seemed all was lost. Cleopatra knew that the middle-aged warrior would take her side. She also knew that if she went strolling back into town to meet with him, her body would arrive at the embalmers before noon. She took advantage of her diminutive size and smuggled herself to Caesar within the rolls of a rug.

Caesar was wooed by her cleverness and beauty. He immediately confirmed their alliance in the bedroom; most likely the queen was a virgin because Ptolemy was too young to consummate their marriage. Virgin or not, she was willing and able. Caesar was famed for his voracious sexual appetite—Cleopatra was apparently sensual enough to fulfill it.

The following morning, Ptolemy stumbled upon his sister in flagrante delicto with the Roman conqueror. A famous story relates that the boy king threw down his crown and whined, "It's not fair!" Ptolemy did not survive long. Under the guise of offering military advice, Caesar insisted Ptolemy lead his Egyptian subjects in battle. The boy's body was found later that day at the bottom of a river, weighed down by his gold armor.

The throne restored, Caesar returned to Rome. He left Cleopatra with a parting gift: a son she named Caesarion, or Little Caesar. Caesar was already married and unable to formally acknowledge his only son. Nonetheless, four years later he invited Cleopatra and Caesarion to Rome. By now, Caesar had conquered much of the world, like Cleopatra's distant relative Alexander the Great. Their love affair reignited, scandalizing Rome. Caesar even installed a statue of Cleopatra as Venus, which did not win him fans. Many thought Caesar would eventually name himself king and marry Cleopatra, thus creating an empire where West would meet East.

All this came to an end in 44 BCE on the infamous ides of March. Caesar's will did not acknowledge Caesarion; instead he left his empire to his grand-nephew Gaius Julius Caesar Octavianus, better known as Octavian. Power struggles soon divided the empire between Octavian and Mark Antony, Caesar's right-hand warrior.

Though Cleopatra fled with her son, Rome soon came a-knockin' at Egypt's door. The savvy queen decided to repeat history, this time with Antony. If she allied with him, their forces could triumph over Octavian to rule the world, which Caesarion would inherit when he came of age.

Like Cleopatra's father, Antony was of a Dionysian bent; like Caesar, he was older and susceptible to the queen's charms. She invited Antony to dinner upon her barge and appeared dressed as a goddess. Locals whispered that Aphrodite was mating with Dionysus. Aphrodite overwhelmed Dionysus with luxurious sensuality: a carpet made of rose petals, a banquet of the finest wines and foods, all served on bejeweled gold plates while guests reclined on embroidered couches. Cleopatra capped the evening by dissolving an expensive pearl in a goblet of vinegar, which she appeared to drink. This spectacle served to illustrate the overwhelming wealth of Egypt that would be at Antony's disposal—if he gave in to the queen's will.

The two lovers brought out the worst in each other. Antony initiated Cleopatra into his Society of the Inimitable Livers, which involved much alcohol, food, and gambling. Cleopatra took advantage of Antony's natural generosity and loyalty. He helped her win new territories, alienating him from the Roman Empire, and agreed to marry her. To do so, Antony abandoned his pregnant wife, who happened to be Octavian's sister—not a smart move. Plutarch wrote that Antony was "besotted with the woman as well as with the wine" and that she controlled him with love potions, a claim that reveals more about the charms of Cleopatra than the truth of the matter.

To create a dynasty of their own, Cleopatra spawned three children with Antony. Antony acknowledged Caesarion as Caesar's son, undermining the legitimacy of Octavian's rule. Not surprisingly, Octavian declared war on them. Fate was not kind: It took time, but Rome's forces thumped Cleopatra and Antony. Their allies abandoned the couple like rats off a sinking ship.

Trapped, Cleopatra and Antony huddled down in Alexandria to await the worst; the Society of Inimitable Livers became the Society of Those Who Die Together. To avoid capture by Octavian, Antony stabbed himself. One legend claims that on the night he died, a strange clamor of horns sounded, then faded away—Dionysus abandoning his own. Cleopatra chose a more elegant method to dispatch herself. She arranged for a basket of figs to be smuggled to her, with two poisonous asps hidden within it.

In death, Cleopatra became Egypt's last pharaoh. Caesarion did not survive to inherit his mother's throne—Octavian decided that two Caesars were one too many and arranged for his murder.

CAUTIONARY MORAL
Choose your allies well, or they will come
back to bite you in the asp.

Empress Wang

23 CE

ittle is known about Empress Wang beyond her birth, her marriages, and her death—even her first name has been lost to history. Even so, one dominant characteristic emerges from these sketchy details: The girl had some serious backbone.

The woman who would become known as Empress Wang was fathered in 8 BCE by Wang Mang, a commander of arms who possessed towering hubris gilded with Confucian idealism. Wang Mang took advantage of the troubled times to become acting regent of China, gaining support by promising the poor an acre of land for every plow. To strengthen his rule, he married his four-year-old daughter to Emperor Ping, who was only three. Little did Wang Mang realize that his plotting would eventually spell doom for the preschool empress.

By the time she was twelve, Empress Wang was a widow—most believe that Wang Mang poisoned Ping's wine when the boy proved to be less than tractable. Wang Mang continued to trade his daughter's hand for power. This time, Empress Wang's husband was a more easily manipulated two-year-old, also in line to the throne. To express her disapproval of her father's actions, Empress Wang refused to attend any imperial functions and swore fealty to her first husband, whom she appears to have genuinely loved and mourned.

Some years later, an uprising ousted Wang Mang from power. Empress Wang realized that no matter whose side she took, she was royally screwed. A solution presented itself when the palace was set on fire by her subjects. Rather than live as her father's puppet, she threw herself into the flames.

CAUTIONARY MORAL
Don't let others' ambitions destroy you.

End-of-Chapter Quiz
or
What We Have Learned So Far

1. Why was Athaliah bad news during biblical times?

○ a. Her mother was Jezebel, queen of the hootchy-kootchy.

○ b. She had a murderous streak as wide as the Red Sea.

○ c. Her recipe for matzo balls was subpar.

○ d. Her name was difficult to pronounce.

2. Which of the following statements is incorrect about Olympias?

○ a. She had the hots for Dionysus and snakes.

○ b. She thought her son, Alexander, was the best thing to hit the Macedonian empire since the wheel.

○ c. She encouraged her husband, Philip, to ratchet up his wife count— polygamy is fun!

○ d. She was played by Angelina Jolie in a *very* long Oliver Stone movie.

3. Why did Amastris wed so often?

○ a. The thrill of the bridal registry.

○ b. She did not believe in premarital sex.

○ c. She had a good divorce lawyer who got her great alimony.

○ d. Survival, baby.

4. Cleopatra and her sisters Berenice and Arsinoe:

○ a. Were one big happy family.

○ b. Wore the same crown size.

○ c. Plotted against one other to grab the throne of Egypt.

○ d. Were caught in flagrante delicto with Marc Antony.

The snake, friend of Dionysus

5. Why was Empress Wang doomed?

○ a. She liked to play with matches.

○ b. Her father valued personal ambition over paternal affection.

○ c. She valued personal integrity over physical survival.

○ d. She didn't know her first name.

CHAPTER TWO

Dancing in the Dark Ages

OUT OF THE MOUTHS OF BABES
It is a pity that we so often succeed in
our endeavors to deceive each other.

Empress Irene

*C*leopatra's choice of death by asp was a media-worthy finale to her notorious reign. It inspired historians to disseminate her story throughout the Western world—an early example of celebrity journalism at its finest— and revved the next generation of queens into action. These women learned from Cleopatra's cautionary saga for better and for worse. Determined to take their fate into their own hands, they were rough, tough, and savvy. Plus they were willing to tango with armies.

The era of the warrior queen spanned the late classical period through the Dark Ages, or early medieval period. One warrior queen conscious of the Cleopatra Effect was Zenobia, who ruled the Palmyrene Empire in the third century. This luscious, clever beauty—descriptions of Zenobia make her sound like a Nigella Lawson generously spiced with cojones— claimed the Egyptian queen as a distant relation through her mother. Unlike Cleopatra, Zenobia survived to tell the tale after waging war. Alas, this was not to be the case for Boudicca, who lived two centuries before Zenobia, and Brunhilde, who lived five centuries after Boudicca. Both Boudicca and Brunhilde were tenacious, charismatic regents. Both also became involved in grudge wars that ultimately led to their destruction.

Dying in battle was bad enough. But by the early sixth century of the Dark Ages, the new-and-not-so-female-friendly Salic law was implemented to complicate the lives of queens throughout Europe. Though it would take some time for the full ramifications of these laws to flower, Salic law was often interpreted to mean that royal women could not inherit property or the right to rule. As such, it would influence dynastic I dos for centuries to come, generating some very unhappy marriages for the sake of preserving power and wealth. Salic law would hang around European courts in various forms until the gilded age of Queen Victoria.

Boudicca

60

ore than a thousand years before William Wallace led his blue painted troops into battle, another warrior made a stand for freedom on Albion's bright shores—a queen named Boudicca. The tale of Boudicca's rise and fall is the stuff from which legends and high-profile films are made. Mel Gibson even optioned her story, inspiring *Variety* magazine to dub his film in development "Braveheart with a bra."

Little is known of Queen Boudicca before she donned armor. Born of royal blood around 30 CE, she was married to Prasutagus, the king of the Iceni tribe of Celtic Britain; the Iceni territories were located in what is now East Anglia. The historian Dio Cassius described the queen in almost superhuman terms. He wrote that she possessed the powerful frame of an Amazon and a mane of fiery-red hair. As for Boudicca's husband, Prasutagus was wealthy and pragmatic. He ruled by kissing up to the Romans in a we'll-scratch-your-back-if-you'll-scratch-ours arrangement; at that time, Britain was overrun by Romans who made life difficult for those who didn't render unto Caesar as demanded.

Everyone got along and even sang a chorus or two of "Kumbaya." However, this peaceful stasis came to a halt when the king died in 60 CE.

At the time of Prasutagus's passing, the couple had two daughters, whose names have been lost to history. The king's will stated that his estate was to be divided in three, between his two daughters and the Roman empire; Boudicca was to act as regent on the princesses' behalf. By doing so, Prasutagus hoped that the Romans would be satisfied with their share and leave his girls alone. But the Romans got greedy and grabbed it all.

Boudicca did not take the theft lying down. The formidable queen hustled to the Roman authorities and gave them a piece of her mind.

OUT OF THE MOUTHS OF BABES
It is not as a woman descended from noble ancestry, but as one of the people that I am avenging lost freedom, my scourged body, the outraged chastity of my daughters. . . . This is a woman's resolve. As for men, they may live and be slaves.

Boudicca

In response, she was flogged and her two daughters raped, stealing their precious virginity. And that was just the *amuse-bouche*: The Romans next claimed the rest of the Iceni lands for themselves.

But Boudicca refused to drown in a puddle of tears. Instead, she grabbed a sword, gathered an army of one hundred thousand soldiers, and went off to kick some serious Roman ass.

Boudicca first attacked Colchester, a Roman colony known back then as Camulodunum. Her forces systematically leveled the city. Years later, archaeologists dated the queen's visit from a layer of red ash. Next up was Londinium, or London. This time, Boudicca's fury extended to the Roman matrons, who were impaled naked on long stakes. Verulamium, modern-day Saint Albans, met a similar fate. Dio Cassius later wrote, "All this ruin was brought upon the Romans by a woman, a fact which in itself caused them the greatest shame."

But the apocalyptic destruction of three cities wasn't enough to slake Boudicca's anger. The queen pushed her luck one last time to wage war in a location probably in the West Midlands. This time, the Roman army got smart. Using a wedge formation, they cornered Boudicca's forces. It is believed that the queen perished here, possibly by her own hand, along with eighty thousand of her troops.

Centuries after her defeat, Boudicca's very distant successor Queen Victoria channeled strength from her namesake—"Boudicca" was Old Welsh for "victorious." The Celtic warrior queen even inspired verse from Tennyson, Victoria's poet laureate. He wrote:

> *So the Queen Boadicea, standing loftily charioted,*
> *Brandishing in her hand a dart and rolling glances lioness-like,*
> *Yell'd and shriek'd between her daughters in her fierce volubility.*

CAUTIONARY MORAL
Have an exit strategy.

Zenobia

274

ike Boudicca, Queen Zenobia of Palmyra chose to lead her people into battle rather than suffer the indignities of Roman dominance. Zenobia lived two hundred years after Boudicca had met her unfortunate end. Presumably she learned from the warrior queen's tragic example, since she wrangled a happier fate.

Zenobia was famed for her sultry beauty, keen intelligence, and athletic prowess. Though she was of Arabian descent, she boasted of being related to Cleopatra through her Egyptian mother, who taught her to speak Egyptian fluently. Zenobia became queen through marriage to Odaenathus, the king of Palmyra. Now part of Syria, the wealthy merchant city of Palmyra served as the rallying point of the Palmyrene Empire and had splintered off from the mighty Roman Empire. Zenobia proved herself her husband's equal on hunting trips but, like the goddess Diana, refused to sleep with him save for the purpose of conception.

After Odaenathus was assassinated in 267, Zenobia decided her personal loss was an opportunity for professional growth—she took charge of the Palmyrene Empire as regent for her young son, Vaballathus. Greedy for power and territory, the queen ambitiously invaded and conquered Egypt,

Zenobia in chains.

57

Syria, and beyond, greatly expanding her empire—and treading on the Roman Empire's toes. Rome took notice and decided to welcome Palmyra back into the fold.

Zenobia's vision for her empire did not include Roman rule. Though an oracle warned that her army would be picked off by Rome like doves by hawks, Zenobia was too stubborn to back down. She personally led her forces into battle on horseback, her beautiful long dark hair rippling behind her on the wind as she charged forward . . . toward disaster.

Palmyra was captured. The Palmyrenes who refused to surrender were executed; those who remained were brought to trial, including the queen.

Ever wily, Zenobia batted her lush eyelashes and testified that she had been led astray by her advisers and didn't know a thing about waging war. The Roman emperor Aurelian didn't buy her story but decided she was worth more alive than dead. In Syria, the queen was shackled to a camel and paraded through the streets as a symbol of Roman victory; in Rome, she was forced to walk in front of Aurelian's triumphal car, her comely body adorned in gold chains weighed down by lustrous jewels.

The *Historia Augusta*, a less-than-reliable third-century document, claims that after this humiliation Zenobia committed suicide in tribute to her ancestress Cleopatra. Another story states she succumbed to disease en route to Rome. However, the most credible accounts suggest that Zenobia's only injury was to her pride. Unlike the queen of the Nile, she wanted to live—even if it was without a throne.

These accounts report that the rest of Zenobia's life was most bourgeois. Aurelian freed her and, as a consolation prize, gave her a villa in Tivoli. The former queen decided that if you can't beat them, join them: She married a Roman senator and spent her remaining years in considerable luxury. In time, she won renown as a philosopher and socialite.

Since nothing more is known of Zenobia, it is assumed that she died peacefully in her sleep after living to a ripe old age and surrounded by her loved ones, like that old lady in *Titanic*.

CAUTIONARY MORAL
It's better to be alive without a crown
than dead with one.

Empress Dowager Hu

528

he life of Empress Dowager Hu was decorated with mind-twisting contradictions. As the concubine of an emperor, she was willing to risk death to bring forth an heir; yet she willingly participated in her son's murder. Despite considering herself a devout Buddhist, she rubbed out those who displeased her without a qualm. One story relates that to eliminate a female competitor, Hu forced her to enter a Buddhist convent where she was welcomed by an assassin; the assassin had been hired by the empress to do her dirty work.

Hu's blood-soaked rise to power began in the early part of sixth-century China, when she was a not so sweet young thing. Her beauty and sharp intelligence gained the appreciative notice of Emperor Xuanwu, who took Hu as one of his concubine consorts. Tradition held that consorts who had given birth to crown princes were executed to avoid future power struggles.

But Hu bucked tradition. When she discovered she was ripe with the heirless emperor's child, she ignored those who warned her to end the pregnancy. Instead, she altruistically argued that it was more important for Xuanwu to have a successor than for her to live.

A BRIEF DIGRESSION

Empress dowager was the official title given to the mother of an underage emperor. Many empress dowagers ruled the nation until their sons reached maturity. Some of them gained so much power that they refused to cede control, leading to unstable political environments. For example, the Empress Dowager Cixi was so skillful with her political machinations that she was able to rule China for four decades during the early twentieth century. Others were content to merely bully their sons' brides into submission—they were the stereotypical mothers-in-law from hell.

Hu's big gamble paid off. After she gave birth to a son named Xiaoming, the emperor spared her life, perhaps out of appreciation for the risk she'd assumed to pass on his genes. However, the power struggles that many feared came to pass five years later, after Xuanwu suddenly died. Five-year-old Xiaoming was crowned emperor and Hu became empress dowager, ruling on behalf of her son.

Empress Dowager Hu was a mixed bag as a regent. She could be extraordinarily generous and progressive—as well as extraordinarily cruel. She set up regional offices where her subjects could safely air their complaints about governmental misdeeds; she also gave away tons of money to build magnificent Buddhist temples. On the other hand, her hair-trigger temper often snapped homicidal over the most piddling offenses.

All children, even sons of empresses, grow up. When Xiaoming turned fifteen, he relieved his mother of her rule. Hu was not pleased. She undermined Xiaoming's reign by utilizing loyal government officials who would follow her will. To limit his mother's influence, Xiaoming arranged for her lover to be executed. Hu retaliated by poisoning Xiaoming to death.

This time Hu had gone too far—even her fiercest allies withdrew their support. To save her skin, the empress hid in a Buddhist convent, where she shaved her head to take the vows of a nun. Nonetheless, her enemies tracked her down. They punished Hu with the only absolute that would stop her.

Empress Hu was drowned in the Yellow River in 528, almost two decades after her son's risky birth. As a posthumous slap, Hu was granted the not so honorable title of Empress Ling—"the unattentive empress."

CAUTIONARY MORAL

To hold on to power, be consistent in your dealings.

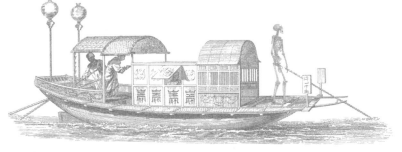

Amalasuntha

535

ucked within a scenic corner of Tuscany, Lake Bolsena lies inside the crater of a dormant volcano. It is a large lake—expansive enough to host several islands, and filled with pristine waters that plunge some five hundred feet down. The legends associated with Lake Bolsena are as dark as the lake is deep. One tells of the fourth-century martyr Christina who, after suffering the usual array of imaginative tortures necessary for beatification, was thrown into the lake while wearing a heavy stone necklace. She instantly bobbed back to the surface cradled within the arms of an angel. Two centuries later, the Ostrogoth queen Amalasuntha was exiled to one of Lake Bolsena's more remote islands. Alas, no heavenly visitor manifested to save her life when she was strangled in her bath one spring morning.

It was a brutal end for a monarch whose main sin was an attempt to import the enlightenment of Roman culture to the war-loving Goths. Consider Amalasuntha a victim of Dark Ages anti-intellectualism.

Amalasuntha was the only daughter of Theodoric the Great, king of the Ostrogoths, and Audofleda, a Frankish princess. By all accounts, Amalasuntha's education was extraordinary. She was educated in Ravenna, where the best of the Byzantine and Roman empires mingled in a high-culture cocktail party. She spoke fluent Latin and Italian as well as her native language. Besides being notoriously literate, the princess was noted for her political acumen and great beauty.

In other words, Amalasuntha had the whole package, if you were a man not intimidated by erudite women. She won the approval of Eutharic, a prince from neighboring Spain; he wed the princess, thus uniting the two

branches of their tribes in holy political might. The contemporary historian Jordanes described Eutharic as "a young man strong in wisdom and valor and health of body." Nonetheless, Eutharic died early in their marriage, leaving her the mother of a son, Athalaric, and a daughter, Matasuentha. A short time later in 526, Amalasuntha's father joined her husband in the grave.

With the two big guys buried, eight-year-old Athalaric inherited the throne, elevating Amalasuntha as his regent until he reached maturity. It is here that most women of her era probably would have lain low to protect their assets—but not Amalasuntha. Instead, she decided to use her lofty position to refine the unwashed Goth masses. The best way to do this? Through King Athalaric, whom she determined would have the best Roman education available.

The public outcry was as if Amalasuntha had switched the channel from WWE to PBS mid-match—for their monarch, the populace wanted a va-va-voom warrior, not some la-di-da student. Her best intentions were criticized as an attack on Goth values. After all, the Goths had conquered the Romans, not the other way around.

Undeterred, the regent hired the most eminent scholars of her time to shape her son's mind. As for Athalaric, he embraced his studies with spring break enthusiasm and drank himself to death by the age of sixteen.

Amalasuntha was smart enough to read the writing on the wall; Jordanes wrote that she "feared she might be despised by the Goths on account of the weakness of her sex." To protect her overeducated self, she arranged for three of her enemies to be murdered and invited her Tuscan cousin Theodahad to keep her company on the throne. This turned out to be a very bad move. Within several months, Theodahad pushed Amalasuntha off the throne and into exile in Tuscany.

Amalasuntha's end arrived quickly. She lasted only a few days on that lonely island on Lake Bolsena before death visited as she bathed. After all, a clean corpse is a godly corpse.

CAUTIONARY MORAL
*Don't let your education
make you stupid.*

Galswintha

568

nce upon a time there were two sisters who were beautiful princesses. The sisters were fathered by Athanagild, the Visigoth king of Spain, and given the fanciful names of Galswintha and Brunhilde. They were raised at the glittering court at Toledo, where it was assumed that they would marry brilliantly and live happily ever after. When the time came, their father agreed for them to wed two powerful brothers, tying the sisters in marriage as well as by blood.

And here is where the two sisters' fairy tale went seriously awry.

Brunhilde, the younger sister, was the first to tie the knot in 567. She married King Sigebert, who ruled the realm of Austrasia, which was part of the Frankish kingdom (now France) ruled by the Merovingian dynasty. Sigebert, aka King Charming, was enchanted by his bride's virtue, comeliness, and intelligence. The couple fell madly in love. As for Galswintha, she drew the short stick. She wed King Charming's brother Chilperic, who ruled Neustria, Austrasia's next-door neighbor in the Frankish kingdom.

Chilperic was renowned as a libertine who had bedded and impregnated more than a few miladies at court; rumor held that he was especially tight

Chilperic with Galswintha's successor. She wasn't as nice as she was pretty.

with his latest concubine, Fredegund, who was originally a serving maid. The historian and cleric Gregory of Tours described Chilperic as "the Nero and Herod of our time." Despite these less-than-stellar portents, Galswintha's father agreed to the match so he could scoop up additional Frankish support for Spain. The king mollified his conscience by asking Chilperic to clean up his act around his daughter.

Galswintha and Chilperic were married in Rouen. Initially Galswintha was received with great honor as queen—Chilperic was delighted with the treasures she had brought in her dowry. However, this felicitious state did not last long. Fredegund reappeared in the king's bed and grabbed every opportunity to harass the new queen. Poor Galswintha begged to return to Toledo, even offering to forfeit her dowry. Chilperic refused.

A year after the wedding, Galswintha was discovered lifeless in her bed—Chilperic, influenced by the urgings of Fredegund, had ordered a slave to strangle his wife. Though the king wept crocodile tears, everyone knew the deal. He also flaunted his passion for his coconspirator, which didn't deter suspicions.

Several days later, the funeral meats coldly furnished the marriage tables—King Chilperic wed Fredegund, making her queen of Neustria.

CAUTIONARY MORAL
Once a rat, always a rat.

THE HOUSE OF MEROVINGIA

or
A Tale of Two Sisters (and Two Brothers)

Two sisters marrying two brothers sounds so downright jovial, like the denouement of a Shakespearean comedy. In this instance, brotherly love proved deadly for both sisters, Galswintha directly and Brunhilde indirectly.

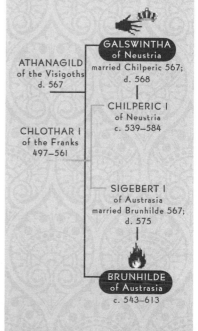

GALSWINTHA
of Neustria
married Chilperic 567;
d. 568

ATHANAGILD
of the Visigoths
d. 567

CHILPERIC I
of Neustria
c. 539–584

CHLOTHAR I
of the Franks
497–561

SIGEBERT I
of Austrasia
married Brunhilde 567;
d. 575

BRUNHILDE
of Austrasia
c. 543–613

Brunhilde

613

he bonds of sisterhood transcend the grave. In the case of Brunhilde of Austrasia, it can also lead to it.

After her sister Galswintha's murder in 568, Brunhilde was transformed from the wife of King Charming into a monarch with a mission—and the mission was revenge. To gain it, the queen of Austrasia incited a forty-year war between her realm and Neustria that made the Hatfields and the McCoys seem downright Merchant-Ivory.

How was a queen able to get armies marching over a victim of domestic violence? Ironically, it was Brunhilde's happy marriage that did the trick. It was easy for her to sway her husband to her will, just as Fredegund's whisperings had prodded Chilperic to uxoricide. It helped that King Charming wasn't too fond of his brother in the first place. Nor were the rest of the Merovingian blue bloods, who joined en masse to dethrone black sheep Chilperic over the murder. One would have considered justice served, but Chilperic soon regained his crown, much to Brunhilde's chagrin.

Every good fairy tale needs a wicked queen—Chilperic's wife, Fredegund, made an exemplary one. As the conflict escalated, she revealed herself to be as unscrupulous in war as she was in peace. At one point, Fredegund sent a clerk to assassinate Brunhilde. When the clerk returned unsuccessful, she had his feet and hands cut off in punishment.

By 575, the war had claimed the life of King Charming—Fredegund persuaded two slaves to attack him with poisoned knives. Then Brunhilde was imprisoned in Rouen. All seemed lost until one of Chilperic's excess sons from his philandering days visited her out of curiosity. Turned out that the queen still retained her allure, so he wed and bedded her. Before the forbidden marriage could be annulled by the church—after all, Brunhilde was his uncle's widow—he helped her escape.

With Brunhilde free again to do as she wished, the war dragged on. As the decades passed, more royals lost their lives. Chilperic, the guy who started it all, was stabbed to death in 584, leaving Fredegund conveniently in charge. Then Fredegund died in 597, presumably of natural causes. Fredegund's son Chlotar proved to be a chip off the old block when he took over his mom's throne. By now, Brunhilde had lost any popularity she may have held—no one remembered the murder of her sister, only the copious bloodshed that had ensued.

In the end, Fredegund triumphed from beyond the grave over her old enemy: The armies of Austrasia and Neustria joined as one to overthrow Brunhilde. King Chlotar II arranged an execution for the conquered queen that would have brought tears of pride to his mother's eyes. After torturing Brunhilde for three days, he paraded her on a camel before the entire army. Her limbs were chained to wild horses, who quartered her, and her remains thrown into a bonfire.

Thus was Brunhilde's spirit conscribed to the great beyond. Hopefully she met Galswintha there, who high-fived her for her filial loyalty.

☠

CAUTIONARY MORAL
To keep your head,
quit while you're ahead.

Queen Brunhilde under stress.

LA MÉTHODE DE MORT

Drawing and Quartering

Call Brunhilde an unlucky exception to the rule: Women and royals usually weren't executed by being drawn and quartered. This procedure was deployed on commoners guilty of various treasonous crimes. Nobles were granted the honor of a speedy death by beheading. Death by being drawn and quartered was far more prevalent in England and her colonies than in Europe during the Dark Ages.

The death was as horrible as it sounds. The condemned were usually hung before being dismembered by sword, rather than by horse—one would hope a much swifter and more merciful route to meeting the grim reaper.

Irene of Byzantium

803

rene of Byzantium was a woman ahead of her time. Instead of using warfare to gain power, she waged a postmodern battle of symbols and images not dissimilar to those on Madison Avenue today. Though Irene's strategy worked on the populace for a while, eventually it became apparent that this empress wore no clothing.

Irene's origins gave little indication of the voracious drive that would make her the the first female ruler of the Byzantine Empire. Born of Greek nobility in 752, one story claims that Irene was an orphan doomed to a quiet life until her beauty caught the eye of Leo IV, the emperor of Byzantium.

A BRIEF DIGRESSION

Icon veneration was controversial in eighth- and ninth-century Byzantium. The iconoclasts believed icons violated the first commandment ban on graven images. The iconophiles found them useful tools for contemplating the divine—they thought icons represented the physicality of God as manifested in Jesus. In 754 the church ruled, "If anyone shall endeavor to represent the forms of the Saints in lifeless pictures with material colors which are of no value (for this notion is vain and introduced by the devil), and does not rather represent their virtues as living images in himself, let him be anathema!" Despite this, people—like Irene—still worshiped icons in secret.

He married her in 769. Two years later, Irene did the good empress thing and provided him with an heir, Constantine. Nevertheless, their marriage was troubled. Irene was an iconophile, which was verboten by the Eastern Orthodox Church. Leo ceased marital relations with the empress after discovering her hidden stash—eternal damnation was far less appealing than the pleasures of the flesh.

Still, Irene harbored secret ambitions, which she was able to fulfill after Leo's unexpected demise in 780. The emperor had taken a sacred crown from Hagia Sophia for

his personal use. Problem was the heavily jeweled crown rubbed his brow until it blistered; the blisters became infected. After Leo's death, Irene arranged for additional pearls to decorate the crown, which she returned to the church in time for display at Christmas mass. She also became regent for ten-year-old Constantine, who was much too young to rule.

Now in charge, Irene restored icon veneration, which pleased her subjects immensely. In another populist move, she cut taxes, which pushed the treasury into the red. As a corrective, she minted and distributed coins bearing her portrait. Though her son was also on them, it was Irene who held the scepter and was labeled *basileus*—emperor.

Not surprisingly, the empress refused to relinquish power when Constantine came of age. He pushed her off the throne in 790 but proved to be an incompetent ruler. Seven years later, Irene took matters back into her own hands. She imprisoned her son and had him blinded, an act considered marginally more merciful than outright assassination.

Nevertheless, Irene's days on the throne were numbered. She was deposed by her finance minister in 802 and exiled to the island of Lesbos. The woman who was once empress spent the remainder of her life there spinning wool for clothing.

CAUTIONARY MORAL
Make sure your style has substance.

LIFE AFTER DEATH

Despite her misdeeds, the Eastern Orthodox Church did not forget all Irene had done to further the restoration of icon veneration. For this, the former empress was beatified as a saint, thus reforming Irene's tarnished public image.

Bust of Irene on an eighth-century coin.

End-of-Chapter Quiz
or
What We Have Learned So Far

1. Why did Boudicca battle the Roman Empire?

○ a. She wanted to prove to her daughters that the Romans were wusses.

○ b. She was tired of converting exchange rates for Roman tourists.

○ c. The Romans got too cozy with her land and her daughters' chastity.

○ d. She knew it was a great branding opportunity for her tribe.

2. To hold on to her throne, Empress Hu was willing to do anything but:

○ a. Plot against her enemies.

○ b. Slip poison into her son's favorite dish.

○ c. Watch her favorite lover get bumped off by her son.

○ d. Cough up lots and lots of dough for her favorite Buddhist temples.

3. Amalasuntha's many talents included:

○ a. The ability to speak several languages fluently.

○ b. A sensitivity to the cultural legacy of the Goths.

○ c. The wisdom to make the most of her time in exile.

○ d. Knowing which scholars were da bomb of her era.

4. What did Brunhilde and Galswintha *not* have in common?

○ a. The same parents.

○ b. The same in-laws.

○ c. The same happily-ever-after marital history.

○ d. The same grudge against Fredegund, that slut.

5. Irene of Byzantium was known for:

○ a. Her affection for icons—religious tchotchkes for the devout home decorator.

○ b. Her sublime skills as a mother.

○ c. Fiscal brilliance to rival a Rockefeller.

○ d. The serenity to accept the things she could not change.

CHAPTER THREE

Middle Age Crisis

OUT OF THE MOUTHS OF BABES

I am much to be pitied both as a queen and as a woman:
When one is fifteen a crown is heavy to wear, and I have
not the liberty of the meanest of my subjects. . . .

Joan of Naples,
via Alexandre Dumas

*O*ne would suspect that, after the travails of the Dark Ages, life could only improve for queens of the later Middle Ages. It didn't. Next in line to ratchet up the royal fatality count were the Crusades and the Black Death (aka the bubonic plague).

To avoid infection by the plague, most blue-blooded females sought sanctuary from the larger populace. Boccaccio's *Decameron* describes one such scenario, where a group of noblemen and -women retreat to an isolated villa to pass the time until the worst of the epidemic passes. Even so, without an emergency broadcasting system in place, there was little to prevent a princess traveling to a distant dynastic alliance from strolling straight into plague territory. Some ended up wearing their bridal veil as a burial shroud; Joan of England, fiancée of Pedro of Castile, was one such unfortunate victim. Feminine vulnerabilities were also made apparent in childbirth, which killed approximately 20 percent of medieval mama wannabes—clearly this was not the age of *Childbirth Without Fear*.

As for the Crusades, royal women were generally more prone to survival than their male counterparts—usually they weren't the ones marching into battle. Nonetheless, Sibyl of Jerusalem chose to participate in the Third Crusade, only to lose her life and daughters as a result. It is hoped that the powers that be appreciated her sacrifice.

While it is unknown how many people died during these religious wars, it is estimated that as many as thirty million folks were killed by the plague—approximately half of Europe's population at that time. That written, marriage proved to be a far more deadly enterprise for many queens. Without divorce readily available, murders were often initiated by unhappy spouses and uppity relatives eager to rid themselves of an unwanted alliance. The deaths of Gertrude of Meran, Blanche of Bourbon, Joan of Naples, and Maria of Hungary all serve as cautionary tales for those eager to embrace nuptial delights.

Urraca of Castile

1126

n 1109 Urraca, the daughter of King Alfonso VI, became the queen of Castille and León; these two kingdoms sat cozily next to each other in what is now Spain.

Until this point, Urraca's sheltered life was filled with the usual princess distractions of getting married and getting knocked up. She was wed as a child to Raymond of Burgundy, with whom she had a son and a daughter before his premature demise in 1107. Becoming queen wasn't even on Urraca's radar, but all this changed when Urraca's only brother was killed in battle in 1108, making the widowed princess heir to the throne. Soon after, her father, King Alfonso VI, went to his eternal reward. Next thing Urraca knew, everyone was addressing her as "your majesty."

Before his death, King Alfonso had arranged for Urraca to exchange vows with another Alfonso—Alfonso I of Aragon. This Alfonso was better known as Alfonso the Battler because of his prowess as a warrior. Problem was Urraca and Alfonso Junior shared the same great-grandfather—the church considered the union too close for comfort. The couple were wed nonetheless, but the ensuing *scandale* pushed the marriage to the breaking point, especially after Alfonso proved to be a battler at home as well as on the battlefield.

Childbirth

Be they of royal or common blood, women of ye olde times considered childbirth a dark passage that could drag both mother and child to early graves. Puerperal fever, a form of blood poisoning linked to unsanitary conditions, was recorded by Hippocrates in ancient Greece. It took until 1847 for the connection between puerperal fever and germs to be made. Viennese physician Ignaz Phillippe Semmelweis noted a dramatic decline in postpartum maternal deaths after he began washing his hands before attending a birth. Afterward, the good Herr Doktor confessed, "God only knows the number of women whom I have consigned prematurely to the grave."

Puerperal fever was Scylla to the Charybdis of obstructed births. Forceps were not introduced until the 1700s, so too many women expired after days of unproductive labor. Sawbones foolhardy enough to attempt a cesarean usually saved the child at the expense of the mother.

Even if a woman survived with a healthy, living child, there was still the torture of labor to endure without an epidural. Many judged these pains punishment for Eve's trespasses in Eden.

But Urraca was tough: The queen dumped Alfonso when she did not promptly conceive an heir by him. One wonders if the reason for their lack of issue went beyond the horrors of domestic abuse. The king was fond of declaring, "The man devoted to war needs the companionship of men, not women."

Urraca and Alfonso's disastrous union was annulled in 1114. Regardless, resentment between the two monarchs continued to simmer. It exploded into a long and bloody war after Alfonso used his finely honed military skills to grab some of his ex-wife's lands. Urraca was woman enough to fight back and, with the aid of her son by her first husband, she emerged victorious.

Urraca proved to be as passionate in love as she was in war. While she never married again, she did enjoy a bevy of friendships with benefits. This ultimately proved to be her Achilles' heel—in the end the woman who had reigned over much of Spain during such tumultuous times was most likely undone by childbirth. The *Historia Compostelana*, an anonymously written history of that era, relates that Urraca got knocked up by a lover and perished in labor.

At the time of her death, the queen had reached the advanced maternal age of forty-six, after reigning more than capably for seventeen years.

CAUTIONARY MORAL
Biology can be a bitch.

Sibyl of Jerusalem

1190

eanwhile, in other parts of the Western Hemisphere, the Crusades were in full swing. These holy wars were initially intended to return the Muslim-occupied lands of Jerusalem and beyond to the dominion of those who followed the Christian faith. However, the Crusades soon became a venue for mercenary knights to seek their fortunes and for the pious to sacrifice their lives, conveniently reducing the population on both counts. Good times.

By the end of the First Crusade in 1099, Jerusalem had been dragged back into the Christian fold, though the holy war festivities would continue for another two centuries. The new-and-improved Kingdom of Jerusalem was set up as a traditional monarchy and began acquiring neighboring territories to flesh out its skeletal realm—an encroachment not unnoticed by border Muslim states. It was into this powder keg of a situation that Sibyl inherited the throne of Jerusalem in 1186.

Queen Sibyl was born around 1160 to Amalric I and Agnes of Courtenay. Amalric became king of Jerusalem in 1162 after his brother died. Interestingly, Sibyl's mother was never crowned queen because the church considered their union incestuous—Amalric and Agnes shared a common great-great-grandfather. The royal marriage was annulled after Amalric became king, though Sibyl's and her brother Baldwin's legitimacy were upheld.

Sibyl's hand in marriage was a hot property, especially after it came out

Gettin' hitched, medieval style.
Adapted from a period manuscript.

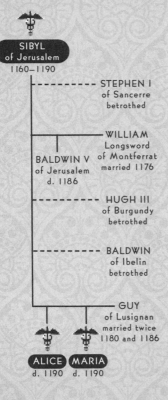

THE SPOUSES OF SIBYL

or

If at First You Don't Succeed

As a ruling monarch, Queen Sibyl was quite the catch on the medieval-era matrimonial market.

SIBYL
of Jerusalem
1160–1190

- - - - - - - - - **STEPHEN I**
of Sancerre
betrothed

———————— **WILLIAM**
Longsword
BALDWIN V of Montferrat
of Jerusalem married 1176
d. 1186

- - - - - - - - - **HUGH III**
of Burgundy
betrothed

- - - - - - - - - **BALDWIN**
of Ibelin
betrothed

———————— **GUY**
of Lusignan
married twice
1180 and 1186

ALICE **MARIA**
d. 1190 d. 1190

that Baldwin had leprosy—ergo, anyone who gained her hand would wind up king of Jerusalem once father and brother bit the dust. Sibyl's marital history took on Liz Taylor proportions as she became engaged, married, widowed, and annulled in varying combinations. She met her soul mate in Guy of Lusignan, whom she wed in 1180. Two daughters soon followed, joining her son, Baldwin V, from an earlier marriage.

Six years later, Amalric and Baldwin the leper were cold in their graves and Sibyl became queen. For numerous reasons, the powers that be decided that Guy was a less than desirable king. They pressured Sibyl to dump him pronto. But the new queen proved to be wily beyond her twentysome-thing years. She agreed to their request, as long as she could choose her next husband. Sibyl remarried Guy before the ink had a chance to dry on the annulment decree.

While all these matrimonial shenanigans were taking place, the Muslims had been united in their outrage by Saladin, sultan of Egypt. A mere year after Sibyl became queen, Saladin successfully invaded Jeru-salem, kicking Sibyl and Guy into exile and setting the stage for the Third Crusade.

Queen Sibyl died in 1190 during the Third Crusade after an epidemic infected most of her military camp. Her two young daughters expired with her.

CAUTIONARY MORAL
When you wage war for God,
you may inherit the kingdom of heaven.

Gertrude of Meran

1213

everal hundred years before Shakespeare wrote "To be or not to be," there was another Queen Gertrude who was not to be. This Gertrude was born in the seaside duchy of Meran and became the wife of Andrew II, the king of Hungary, at the beginning of the thirteenth century. But like Hamlet's ill-starred mother, she became entangled in unseen conspiracies that would lead to the grave.

Much of Gertrude's misfortune can be traced to timing. She married into the Hungarian nobility during a tricky period of transition. Her husband, Andrew, was in the midst of transferring lands from the crown to the people, a process that had begun during his predecessor's reign. Some of the lesser nobles became impatient for their share and perceived any favor shown to another as a slight against their rights. Gertrude took the fall after several of her relatives were granted high positions at court. True, Andrew was the crown behind the appointments, but it mattered not. Several jealous Hungarian aristocrats expressed their extreme displeasure by murdering the queen in 1213.

One account states Gertrude was assaulted while out hunting. Andrew was unable to protect her, since he was off squelching a rebellion in neighboring

Béla IV. A Hamlet with a difference.

territories. At the time of her demise, the queen was only twenty-eight years old, but had already fulfilled her biological duty by giving birth to five children. They included an heir, Béla IV, and two daughters to be married off, Anna Maria and Elisabeth.

Gertrude's murderers were not punished until more than thirty years later. At the time of her death, King Andrew simply shrugged off the loss and married again—the situation was too politically explosive to seek justice. However, it was a different story after 1235, when Andrew died and Béla took over the throne of Hungary.

King Béla was Hamlet with a difference. While he was slow at avenging his mother's murder, he was effective—he tracked down her murderers and punished them. Béla ruled Hungary until his death in 1270, more than half a century after Gertrude had been sacrificed for royal intrigue.

CAUTIONARY MORAL
*Justice served late
doesn't remedy death served early.*

LIFE AFTER DEATH

Gertrude's daughter Elisabeth of Hungary was as pious as her brother Béla was patient. Four years after her death in 1231, she was canonized.

Elisabeth spent her childhood apart from her mother. At the age of four, she was betrothed to Louis, the Landgrave of Thuringia, and sent to live in his court. The couple was very happy together, but when Louis died during the Fifth Crusade, Elisabeth devoted herself to good works and entered a convent. Her story inspired another Hungarian, Franz Liszt, to compose an oratorio.

The miracle of the roses: To avoid having her charity work discovered, St. Elisabeth tranformed bread for the poor into roses for the rich. Liszt used the incident in his oratorio of her life.

Oghul Ghaimish

1248

The Mongol Empire was spread over the largest contiguous land mass in history. At its height, it held an estimated one hundred million subjects—about a third of the current population of the United States. The territory that comprised the empire encompassed the harshest environments in the world. Temperatures drop below 30 degrees Fahrenheit in the winter and spike to over 100 in the summer. Despite this, its location made it economically valuable. The Silk Road wound through the heart of the empire, channeling rich resources from China to Rome.

In other words, becoming the great khan, or emperor, of the Mongol Empire went far beyond simply bossing people around—it was about controlling the wealth of nations.

When Oghul Ghaimish grabbed the throne of the Mongol Empire, it was as if Melinda Gates made herself chairwoman of Microsoft without first checking in with the shareholders. Like Melinda, Oghul had connections: Her husband, Güyük, a grandson of Genghis Khan, ruled the empire until his death from alcoholism at the age of forty-two in 1248. She had familial precedent: Güyük's mother, Töregene Khatun, served as regent for five years before amassing enough political might to transition her son onto the throne.

Unlike Töregene, Oghul's reign lasted only a few months. A nasty power struggle

The Mongols were famed as fierce warriors.

A BRIEF DIGRESSION

What makes black magic different from white or other types of magic? It's all about intention. With black magic, the sorcerer manipulates forces or spirits to perform his will without consideration of how it could affect or harm others. While white magic may also be used for selfish reasons, it cannot be employed to injure another.

As for Oghul herself, for good or ill, one could assume that the Mongolian khan knew something of magic since she was of royal origin. In *The Golden Bough*, an encyclopedic treatise on the origins of magic and religion, Sir James Frazer writes that in many early societies "the king is frequently a magician as well as a priest; indeed he appears to have often attained to power by virtue of his supposed proficiency in the black or white art."

immediately erupted over the question of who should be the next ruler, which many thought should be someone other than the previous great khan's widow.

Oghul's primary opposition came from another grandson of Genghis Khan, Möngke, who called for a general election. To gain the throne, Möngke called in all his political favors. Oghul lost by a single vote.

But this not so decisive victory wasn't enough for Möngke and his band of supporters. To completely disempower Oghul, they played the witch card: They accused her of employing black magic against the newly elected ruler.

The former regent was dragged to court and, after a sham trial, she was condemned to death. Perhaps to avoid the appearance of excessive force, the court allowed Oghul to commit suicide. It is unknown what method she chose.

CAUTIONARY MORAL
Look before you leap onto the throne.

Theodora of Trebizond

1285

f you ruled an empire for just one year, what would you do? This was the situation presented to Empress Theodora, who reigned over Trebizond for one brief, giddy trip around the sun.

Trebizond was a Hellenistic state that emerged from the Byzantine Empire after the Fourth Crusade's sacking of Constantinople in 1204. Because Trebizond was on the coast of the Black Sea, it became an important stop on the Silk Road trade route to Asia. Beyond this, the empire was at the mercy of forces beyond its control—by 1461, it had been obliterated by the Ottomans. Though Trebizond is now part of modern-day Turkey, back in Theodora's time it was considered the last hurrah of the glorious Greek empire.

During the sunset of the thirteenth century, Theodora was born the daughter of Emperor Manuel I and his second wife, a Georgian princess. After her father's death in 1263, Theodora's two older brothers, Andronikos and George, ruled Trebizond. By 1282, they were history: Andronikos was dead, George deposed by Mongol forces unrelated to Oghul Ghaimish.

Next up on the throne was Theodora's younger half brother, John. This time, the princess did not wait around twiddling her thumbs. When John took off for Constantinople in 1284 to get married, she used her mother's Georgian connections to seize the throne. Alas, their help was not enough—brother John deposed her one year later, putting the empress out of commission.

Theodora's main accomplishment during her truncated reign was to have minted her own coins. Given the importance of Trebizond as a trade center, presumably these coins reached a wide circulation and outlasted her

Religious Orders

In Theodora's time and beyond, noblewomen faced two possible life plans (if they were allowed to choose at all): marry a man or marry Jesus. Some independent of mind and wealth picked the son of God over producing sons, finding a convent's conscribed freedoms and intellectually vigorous environment more attractive than some old guy with land. After all, nuns could read, write, and even practice an art or two.

Most brides of Christ came from money, since a dowry was de rigueur to woo the church. While some girls were promised from childhood, others took religious orders when widowed. A few even sought sanctuary from toxic political environments. Hidden away from the world under a wimple, a deposed queen couldn't plot her return to power—or could she?

The reality wasn't so romantic.

time on the throne. Like her precursor Irene, who ruled the Byzantine Empire a half century earlier, Theodora understood the importance of symbols. It is difficult to imagine what else she might have done had she ruled longer.

The once and past empress was fortunate that her brother did not execute her after he returned to Trebizond to regain his crown. Instead, Theodora experienced the imprisonment of religious orders. Since history tells us little more of her, it is assumed she spent the remainder of her life as a bride of Christ.

☠

CAUTIONARY MORAL
*To save your life,
get thee to a nunnery.*

Blanche of Bourbon

1361

he princess trapped in the tower is a theme that's launched a thousand fairy tales. In most of these *contes des fées*, the princess winds up rescued by a prince or a king, who eagerly claims her as his bride. But what happens when the princess is imprisoned by the king himself? Can there still be a happy ending?

In the case of Blanche of Bourbon, the answer was a resounding *non*. Though the French princess was renowned for her piety and comeliness, any happiness her future might have held was destroyed when her father, the Duke of Bourbon, decided to marry her to King Pedro of Castile.

On paper, the match must have looked fabulous; in real life, it was a mess. Yes, Blanche would become a queen—definitely an upgrade from princess. Yes, the couple was age appropriate—Blanche was a virginal fourteen and Pedro a studly eighteen. But Castile was a serpent's nest of war because Pedro's father had spawned seven bastards and accorded them too much power. To hold his throne, Pedro spent most of his free time killing off unsupportive relatives. These not so nice actions earned him the *nom de royale* of Pedro the Cruel.

The other portents for the match were equally bleak. The king's previous

Pedro the not so nice.

fiancée, Princess Joan of England, had succumbed to the Black Death en route to marry him. Rumor held that she lucked out, since Pedro was already married—either an inconvenient impediment or a damnable sin, depending on how you looked at it.

Blanche's parents ignored the negative advertising and hoped for the best. In 1353, the princess dutifully traveled from France to Castile to wed the king. On her arrival, Pedro let Blanche cool her heels for several months; he was too busy canoodling with his mistress, Maria de Padilla, to welcome her. When the

Were their aims true?

king finally did deign to make an appearance, he was less than cordial to Blanche—but he married her anyway.

Pedro's strong aversion to Blanche puzzled his contemporaries, for the princess was no slouch in the charm department. The only explanation they could devise was that Maria had bewitched Pedro with evil spells. Yet Voltaire writes that the teenage princess "had fallen in love with the grand master of St. Jago, one of those very bastards who had waged war against him." If this was true—frankly it seems out of character for Blanche—it reveals that she was more romantic than she was savvy. Fooling around with her fiancé's half brother wasn't the best way to encourage nuptial bliss.

In either case, Pedro overreacted by imprisoning his new wife in the famously fortified castle of Arevalo. Though Queen Blanche won much sympathy for her cruel plight, no one was able to rescue her. Eight years later, Pedro arranged for her death.

How was Blanche murdered? One story relates that Blanche was poisoned; another claims that Pedro sent a crossbowman to assassinate her. In either case, the queen's reign was over. At the time of her demise, Blanche was twenty-two years old and had been trapped in that tower for more than a third of her life.

As for Pedro the Cruel, his end reflected the violence of his life. After reigning acrimoniously for twenty years, he was beheaded by one of his illegitimate half brothers.

☠

CAUTIONARY MORAL
Truth and advertising aren't always strangers.

Joan I of Naples

1382

pousal murder, aka mariticide, wasn't just for morally corrupt kings. By the time Blanche had been sentenced to death by wedlock, her distant cousin Joan had already bumped off her starter husband to better claim the throne of Naples. It was an ignominious start to a reign that would ultimately include exile, plague, and even a brothel.

The rule of Queen Joan initially held great promise—both Boccaccio and Petrarch praised her beauty, intelligence, and politesse. Joan was born in Anjou in 1328 bearing an illustrious pedigree: She was the niece of Phillip VI, the king of France, and the granddaughter of the king of Naples, better known as Robert the Wise. Robert made the girl his sole heir when her father died soon after her birth. To keep it in the family, Joan was betrothed at seven to her second cousin Andrew, a six-year-old Hungarian prince.

Nine years later on his deathbed, Robert the Wise bequeathed the throne of Naples to Andrew, a move that turned out not to be so wise. In doing so, he seriously misread the desires of the populace, who rioted to make Joan their monarch. Voltaire wrote that Andrew "disgusted the Neapolitans by his gross manners, intemperance, and drunkenness." Within two years' time, the king was garroted with a silk cord in the palace.

Joan was accused of her husband's murder. One account claimed that Joan overheard the murder but did not call for help or exhibit distress, which was considered damning evidence of her culpability. In his recounting of her trial, Alexandre Dumas wrote, "An angel soiled by crime, she lied like Satan himself. . . ." The queen got off scot-free. Nevertheless, the damage was done—Andrew's death aroused the ire of his older brother, Louis I of Hungary, which would have fatal repercussions.

As queen, Joan was known for such accomplishments as establishing a large brothel in Avignon for use by the nobility; she was also the countess of Provence by birth. Despite the stench of hellfire lingering about her skirts, Joan tempted fate by marrying another cousin. To gain the pope's approval for the consanguineous union, Joan sold Avignon to the church, plunging area prostitutes into unemployment.

Papal favor or no, Joan and her new hubby were forced to flee Naples after King Louis sent his army marching in. The couple lived as expats in Provence until the Black Death arrived in Naples, persuading the Hungarians to leave town. Joan's triumphant return and coronation were celebrated within L'Incoronata, a cathedral built for the occasion and decorated with frescoes by a student of Giotto. Nonetheless, the queen's crown was unstable—King Louis continued threatening Naples for another three decades.

In 1381, Hungarian forces finally deposed Joan. A year later, karma paid a visit to Joan in prison. She was strangled, suffering the same fate as her first husband.

CAUTIONARY MORAL
If you tarry with crime, you may become a victim.

LIFE AFTER DEATH

Alexandre Dumas, the nineteenth-century author of such swashbucklers as *The Three Musketeers*, purloined the life of Joan for an entry in his *Celebrated Crimes* series. Dumas romanticized the murderous monarch as a beautiful but tortured victim of others' Machiavellian machinations. Other historical figures presented in *Celebrated Crimes* included Lucretia Borgia—Joan was in good company.

Joan, from a period manuscript.

Maria of Hungary

1395

y kicking Joan off her throne, King Louis of Hungary enlarged his considerable holdings to include Naples. This made a tidy inheritance for his eldest daughter, Maria. Alas, it also encouraged her premature demise.

To be fair, Louis had only the best intentions for Maria. He was an older father—the king was forty-five, a veritable medieval-era geriatric when Maria was born—so he did not dally to settle her future, especially since he had no male heir. Louis betrothed Maria as a child to the teenaged Sigismund of Luxemburg. Sigismund was in line to become the Holy Roman Emperor; the union would settle the long-term tension that sizzled between the two families, hopefully granting Maria a peaceful reign. Louis intended that Maria would rule Hungary with Sigismund's help. However, the young'un had ambitions of his own. By age thirteen, Sigismund had already been called on the carpet for scheming in foreign lands.

In 1382, six months after his henchmen had killed Joan, Louis died of natural causes. Queen Maria was only ten, so her mother, Elisabeth of Bosnia, served as her regent. Nonetheless, Maria's marriage to Sigismund was solemnized in 1385. Elisabeth's reign was unnaturally truncated—she was

Maria of Hungary. A damsel in distress.

strangled in front of her daughter in 1387. Though the murder occurred during a kidnapping by a cartel of rebellious nobles, word on the street was that the assassination was ordered by Sigismund, who didn't want a mother-in-law to interfere with his quest for power.

Maria was appropriately freaked. Afterward, the unhappy couple led separate lives with separate courts. Maria allowed Sigismund to rule as he wished.

A decade later, Maria died after a suspicious riding accident while heavily pregnant—take a guess whom most people believed ordered the hit. Since the queen was estranged from her husband, one wonders if Sigismund was the father. Because Maria conveniently died before giving birth, there was no surviving issue to complicate Sigismund's one-man rule.

The crown Sigismund won at Maria's expense brought him more trouble as the decades passed. The king by coup ruled Hungary for fifty very long years, most of which were filled with cheerless fighting, dynastic conspiracies, and copious bloodshed. By dint of survival, Sigismund expanded his powers to become king of Romans and Bohemia and, finally, Holy Roman Emperor in 1433. Four years later, Sigismund met his judgment day at the advanced age of sixty-nine.

CAUTIONARY MORAL
Be wary of others' plans
and the role you may play in them.

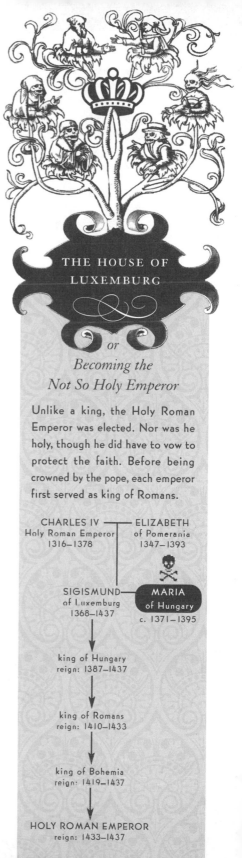

THE HOUSE OF LUXEMBURG

or
Becoming the
Not So Holy Emperor

Unlike a king, the Holy Roman Emperor was elected. Nor was he holy, though he did have to vow to protect the faith. Before being crowned by the pope, each emperor first served as king of Romans.

CHARLES IV	ELIZABETH
Holy Roman Emperor 1316–1378	of Pomerania 1347–1393

SIGISMUND	MARIA
of Luxemburg 1368–1437	of Hungary c. 1371–1395

king of Hungary
reign: 1387–1437

king of Romans
reign: 1410–1433

king of Bohemia
reign: 1419–1437

HOLY ROMAN EMPEROR
reign: 1433–1437

End-of-Chapter Quiz
or
What We Have Learned So Far

1. Which of the following were a danger to medieval queens?

○ a. The bubonic plague, aka the Black Death.

○ b. Scary husbands, like that guy in *Sleeping with the Enemy*.

○ c. Getting knocked up.

○ d. God, Country, and the Crusades.

2. Theodora of Trebizond ended her reign:

○ a. Dangling from the gallows.

○ b. Tying the knot with Christ.

○ c. Light of heart but heavy with memories.

○ d. With more regrets than there are stars in the night sky.

*Just your basic
Black Death.*

3. What was Oghul Ghaimish's claim to the Mongol Empire throne?

○ a. She was regent for her unborn child.

○ b. She completed the Mongolian leadership training course.

○ c. She was succeeding her hubby, who was the previous Great Khan.

○ d. She had chutzpah, baby.

4. Why was Blanche of Bourbon's husband, Pedro, so cruel?

○ a. He was overcompensating for his insecurities.

○ b. He found Blanche less than enchanting.

○ c. He was anticipating the marquis de Sade.

○ d. His parents sent him to military school instead of pottery camp.

5. What did Joan of Naples achieve during her reign?

○ a. She invented Neapolitan ice cream.

○ b. She got away with royal perjury.

○ c. She founded a state-supported brothel in Avignon.

○ d. She lobbied for the public acceptance of mariticide.

ANSWER KEY

1, all of the above. 2, b: We don't know what regrets or memories she took with her to the convent. 3, c. 4, b: Based on how he treated Blanche. 5, c: Trick question. We don't know for sure if Joan lied. To the best of our knowledge, mariticide isn't accepted anywhere.

CHAPTER FOUR

Renaissance Revels

OUT OF THE MOUTHS OF BABES
Commend me to his Majesty, and tell him that he has ever been
constant in his career of advancing me. From a private gentlewoman
he made me a marchioness, from a marchioness a Queen;
and now that he has no higher degree of honour left, he gives
my innocence the crown of martyrdom as a saint in heaven.

Anne Boleyn

The humanist glories of the Renaissance did not extend to the royal women of this era. During this dangerous period, there were two primary forces threatening to push queens off their thrones: infertility and religion.

England was an especially treacherous place for queens, four of whom lost their lives after embracing King Henry VIII as husband. Henry married a total of six times in hopes of scoring a male heir. The king, in his infinite wisdom, judged his first wife, Catherine of Aragon, infertile when she proved incapable of giving birth to a son who could live past infancy.

Ironically, it may have been Catherine of Aragon's surplus of piety that contributed to her woes. A devout Catholic, Catherine fasted to win God's favor—lack of male issue was believed to be punishment for one's sins—which most likely affected her menstrual cycles, making conception problematic at best.

Aside from religion, what were other popular cures for infertility? Since there were no reproductive endocrinologists at this time, remedies leaned toward the DIY variety. These included limiting intercourse, increasing foreplay, uterine fumigation (as unpleasant as it sounds), and elaborate herbal remedies that were inserted into the vagina; one such concoction consisted of galangal, marjoram, and mushrooms (presumably not of the hallucinogenic variety). Conceiving a boy was a whole other ball of wax. Some advised that the couple should gaze into each others' eyes while they mated, an act that supposedly balanced their bodily humors.

To shed Catherine as his spouse, Henry pioneered the use of divorce, founding a new and Protestant church in the process. Afterward, the king fell back on beheading as his preferred *méthode de mort*—dead wives were less trouble when it came to remarrying.

Henry's new church led to years of religious struggles and royal fatalities beyond his reign. After the king's death, both Jane Grey and Mary, Queen of Scots, lost their heads for God and England; Jane was Protestant and Mary, Catholic. On the Continent, Jeanne of Navarre was also entrenched in the Protestant struggle, which may have led to her demise.

In other parts of the globe, queens lost their thrones because of maternal death, insanity, and inbreeding—not necessarily in that order. ✍

Catherine of Aragon

1536

ity poor Catherine of Aragon. As soon as she was born in 1485, it was clear what her fate would be: an imperial womb for sale. Even her choice of royal badge not so subtly reflected this. Catherine selected the pomegranate, an ancient symbol of feminine fertility. The queen's fortunes would rise and fall based on the unpredictability of her menstrual cycles—as would those of countless others.

Catherine was the youngest and prettiest of the four daughters born to Isabella and Ferdinand, Spain's power couple. By the time Catherine was three, her parents had already decided her future: She would wed Arthur, the two-year-old Prince of Wales, to buy an alliance between England and Spain. Over a decade passed before the little princess journeyed to England to marry, accompanied by a dowry of 200,000 crowns; another 200,000 was to be paid later. Catherine was led down the aisle by Arthur's younger brother, Henry, who threw off his robe to dance wildly at the reception.

The joy at the wedding did not last long: Arthur died suddenly four months later. According to Catherine, since they were too young to consummate the marriage, the pomegranate remained untouched. At the age of sixteen, she was a widow in a distant land. Arthur's father took the opportunity to squeeze Ferdinand for the second part of Catherine's dowry; Ferdinand refused to pay, abandoning Catherine to genteel poverty. Seven years passed before Arthur's dancing brother, now King Henry VIII, stepped up to the plate and married her, rescuing her from royal limbo.

How was Henry able to marry his brother's widow? Church law prohibited it based on a passage from the Book of Leviticus: "And if a man shall take his brother's wife, it is an unclean thing . . . they shall be childless." But Henry took Catherine at her chaste word and received a papal dispensation. Scorning the public glitz of Catherine's first wedding, the slightly scandalous

THE HOUSE OF TUDOR, PART I

or

When Love Leads to Death

Henry Tudor had more wives than most of his contemporaries had horses—and their horses had safer lives. Here's a diagram for telling those Catherines and Annes apart.

HENRY VIII
1491–1547

CATHERINE of Aragon
1485–1536

MARY I
1516–1558

ANNE BOLEYN
d. 1536

ELIZABETH I
1533–1603

JANE SEYMOUR
d. 1537

EDWARD VI
1537–1553

ANNE of Cleves
1515–1557

CATHERINE HOWARD
d. 1542

CATHERINE PARR
d. 1548

couple wed in private. Henry had saved Catherine from an uncertain fate to make her queen—she would always love him for this.

Initially, Henry and Catherine were happy. But though three royal sons arrived, none of them survived. Twenty-four years of marriage, many pregnancies, and one living daughter—Mary—later, Henry decided that Leviticus was right. Behind Catherine's back, he petitioned the pope unsuccessfully for another dispensation, this one to annul his marriage so he could wed again for a male heir.

Catherine caught wind of this. She confronted Henry with a tear-filled testimony: "I take God and all the world to witness that I have been to you a true, humble, and obedient wife. . . . I was a true maid, without touch of man." Henry did not refute her. But his mind was made up.

Henry offered Catherine the refuge of the convent as an easy out. But the heartbroken queen refused. She wasn't only fighting for herself—she was protecting Mary's royal claim, since if the marriage was annulled, the princess would be rendered illegitimate. Henry responded by thumbing his nose at Rome and called quits on the marriage himself. He moved Catherine to a faraway castle, where she remained a prisoner until her death three years later. Her autopsy revealed that her heart was as black and misshapen as a dried pomegranate.

CAUTIONARY MORAL
Marrying your husband's brother
is dangerous business.

Anne Boleyn

1536

enry VIII had a not so secret reason for pushing Catherine of Aragon aside: He lusted after Anne Boleyn, whose womb was presumably more receptive to his seed. However, the fate of Henry's first wife was gentler than the fate of his second. Anne was granted the dubious honor of being the first English queen to be publicly executed. This was quite a comedown for a woman who had initially won much attention at the English court for her refined manners and beauty.

Though born in England, Anne spent her formative years on the Continent as a lady-in-waiting to Margaret of Austria and Queen Claude of France. This time abroad polished Anne into a sophisticated woman able to converse wittily in French, dance with élan, and flirt in the best courtly love tradition, where you promise everything but grant nothing. Her unusual dark hair and sultry eyes made her stand out—Anne Boleyn was Tudor England's Angelina Jolie amid a sea of Reese Witherspoons.

Anne returned to England from France in 1521 to marry her father's choice of a groom. But the engagement was brought to a grinding halt for unknown reasons. Again, Anne was sent to court to serve a queen, this time England's Catherine of Aragon. More happily, she fell in love.

The object of Anne's affection was Henry Percy, who was considered a catch since he would inherit an earldom. They became secretly engaged, but secrets did not last long at court. Their marriage was forbidden by the powers that be—there was someone else who wanted Anne, a Henry more powerful than Henry Percy. And what Henry Tudor wanted, Henry got.

Anne never had a chance—Henry stalked her like prey, ignoring her refusals. If it had been modern times, the king would have been slapped with a whopper of a sexual harassment suit. To protect herself, all Anne could do was apply *The Rules*.

The Rules was a popular book from the 1990s that took a page from Anne's courtship philosophy. One of The Rules' authors ended up divorced—it's fortunate for her that she wasn't married to Henry VIII. Anne's story suggests that when it comes to playing hard to get, not much has changed over the years.

Anne's rule number one was don't put out. Rule number two was hold out for the big gold ring. After all, Anne had a front row seat for what happens when a girl doesn't follow the Rules: her sister, Mary, had been the king's mistress and was rewarded with two bastards for her efforts.

Anne was smarter than this—and smarting from the king's ending of her engagement. She determined to make Henry pay by granting her the ultimate favor of the crown.

It took Henry seven years to disentangle himself from Catherine of Aragon to marry Anne—long, tumultuous years that involved papal entreaties, courtroom dances, bribes to Rome, and the death of a cardinal. To gain Anne's hand, Henry eventually resolved that he, as king, was England's absolute religious authority, not some guy in a funny hat in Rome. Henry installed a puppet cardinal in Canterbury who was willing to grant the divorce. Not surprisingly, the king's decision led to his excommunication. It also sent seismic waves throughout Europe, since it effectively sanctioned Martin Luther's Reformation—man no longer required a priest to win God's grace.

Amazingly, during these seven years Anne refused to sleep with Henry until just before their marriage. But she conceived quickly; by her coronation in 1533, her belly was already swollen with child. It is difficult to ascertain exactly when and if Anne fell in love with Henry. Maybe power was an aphrodisiac; maybe she was trying to

Anne pleading for her life before Henry VIII. The reality was rather different. Once Henry decided he'd had enough of Anne, he refused to ever see her again.

make the best of the inevitable. She once admitted, "I never wished to choose the King in my heart." One theory suggests that Anne believed God had chosen her to be queen. She saw herself like Queen Esther, reforming a corrupt church by influencing a besotted monarch. She even encouraged the translation of the Bible into English, so ordinary people could read it without a priest.

Anne's pregnancy resulted in the birth of a daughter, Elizabeth. Soon after, Henry admitted that he believed Anne had used witchcraft to capture his heart—clearly the bloom was already off the rose. Two stillborn sons later, the king sprang into action.

When the king was seriously injured during a jousting match, someone overheard Anne hysterically wonder what would happen if Henry died. Henry decided this amounted to a treasonous plot to kill him. He also claimed Anne had messed around with numerous men, including her brother.

A sham trial resulted in a verdict of death by burning or beheading—the choice was Henry's pleasure. He showed mercy and chose beheading. Strangely enough, Anne's jury included Henry Percy, who was forced to vote for her conviction.

Anne Boleyn was beheaded in 1536. Like Catherine of Aragon, Anne wagered much on her womb and lost. However, Anne's legacy lived on through her illustrious daughter, Elizabeth I.

CAUTIONARY MORAL
There are no Rules for love.

Beheading

Beheading is a quick and effective way to end a life—provided the executioner is skilled. When Mary Stuart marched to the chopping block, it took three ax blows to sever her head; she remained conscious for the first two. Some believe that the executioner deliberately botched the job to prolong her suffering—though one wonders if nerves at dispatching such an illustrious personage to the next life played a part.

Beheading has been utilized worldwide since ancient times. During Henry's era, the condemned were usually blindfolded after they made a pious last statement that included forgiveness of the executioner and praise for the monarch. Next, they placed their necks upon the block; in the case of women, sometimes someone held their hair to the front, to steady them for the blow to come.

Though an ax was traditionally used, Henry sent for a French swordsman to execute Anne; it was rumored that he was so skilled that she would feel no pain. Anne quipped, "He shall not have much trouble, for I have a little neck." The queen was killed with a single sword stroke while kneeling upright midprayer.

Jane Seymour

1537

redictably, Henry VIII went shopping among his wife's employees for his third queen. This time the lucky winner was Jane Seymour.

Jane served as lady-in-waiting to both Catherine of Aragon and Anne Boleyn. Aside from waiting to replace her employer, what exactly did a lady-in-waiting do? During Jane's lifetime, their duties included dressing the queen, readying her for bed, and even wiping her mouth. There were a lot of them, too—over a hundred ladies served Catherine of Aragon.

By the time the king noticed Jane, she was well into her late twenties, a veritable Renaissance spinster. Soon after his marriage to Anne, Henry sent Jane a purse of gold sovereigns. She was wise enough to send it back with a canny message. Jane dramatically threw herself on her knees and begged the king to remember that she had "no greater riches in the world than her honour . . . ; if he wished to make her some present in money she begged it might be when God enabled her to make some honourable match." In other words, Jane stole a play from Queen Anne's playbook. And it worked.

Henry wasted no time in wedding Jane. While Anne was on her knees awaiting the executioner's sword, the king was publicly celebrating his engagement to Jane. The public did not approve. Despite this, the couple waited only eleven days after Anne's execution to marry. Henry, having been burned twice, decided to postpone Jane's coronation until after she coughed up a son.

After the brilliant and beautiful but tempestuous Anne Boleyn, Henry found Jane a soothing change. Jane was plain and boring—a pallid Mrs. de Winter to Anne's vibrant but dead Rebecca. One courtier described Queen Jane as being of "middle height and nobody thinks she has much beauty. Her complexion is so whitish that she may be called rather pale." If Jane had any spunk, she learned to suppress it early in their marriage. After the only time she challenged Henry, he reminded her what had happened to his first two wives, effectively squelching future differences. Some believe that Henry was encouraged to wed Jane by those sympathetic to the Catholic Church; the queen was known for her pious adherence to traditional beliefs. If this was true, she was unable to influence him greatly.

Like a good doormat, Jane chose as her motto "Bound to serve and obey." Which she did—unlike Henry's two previous queens, she gave him his long-desired male heir, who was conceived eight months after their nuptials. However, she did not emerge unscathed. Jane Seymour died of postnatal complications three weeks after the birth of Edward VI in 1537.

CAUTIONARY MORAL
Before you usurp your employer,
consider the downside.

LIFE AFTER DEATH

Henry deemed Jane his only "true wife," presumably because she provided him with an heir and then died before he tired of her. He arranged to be buried next to her. As for his son Edward, he already knew Greek and Latin by his seventh birthday. Alas, Edward's brain was stronger than his body—he died at the age of fifteen from tuberculosis.

Portrait of Edward VI
as a cute baby.

Catherine Howard

1542

I f the definition of insanity is doing the same thing repeatedly while expecting a different outcome, Henry VIII was certifiable. As he had with wives number two and three, Henry plucked his fifth wife, Catherine Howard, from his consorts' ladies-in-waiting. But crazy as he was, Henry had good reason to shop local: No one else would marry him.

After the demise of Jane Seymour, the king tried to choose a bride for political advantage among Europe's most eligible princesses. Most demurred—because of the deaths of his first three queens, Henry had acquired the reputation of a blue-blooded Bluebeard. One reluctant candidate was Christina of Milan. She reportedly told Henry that if she had two heads, she would gladly give him one. Anne of Cleves, a princess from Germany, bravely embraced Scheherazade as her role model and decided she was up to the challenge. Fortunately for Anne No. 2, Henry only annulled their marriage after declaring her sexually repulsive—he simply couldn't get it up for her.

Then came Catherine No. 2. No fancy European princess, Catherine Howard was a party girl newly arrived from the provinces. She was also cousin to Anne Boleyn, whose fate she would soon share. Unlike

The rose too easily pruned.

OUT OF THE MOUTHS OF BABES

I am faithful to the King and would never wish harm upon him. I will seek his mercy, but not by admitting to these treacherous lies.

Catherine Howard

his first Catherine, this Catherine was young, giddy, and uncomplicated. Unlike Anne No. 2, Henry had no problems performing with her.

The king was never so pleased with a wife. He affectionately called her "the rose without a thorn." However, this rose could not be loyal to any gardener: Catherine's past sexual history was known to be colorful. But Henry was so enthralled he never considered the origins of her bedroom talents.

By the time of Catherine and Henry's wedding in 1540, the king had long lost any semblance of health. He was around thirty years older than his young queen and weighed more than 350 pounds. He had a pus-filled wound in his leg that required daily draining. Henry was no dreamboat a hot-to-trot woman barely out of adolescence would lust for.

Though Catherine was hardly innocent, she was shockingly unschooled in the ways of monarchy. She believed that, after a suitable interval, she could choose a lover more suited to her tastes; perhaps the pomp and circumstance of the throne enticed the young queen into thinking that she had the droit de madame to do as she wished.

Old habits die hard. It wasn't long before Catherine indulged in a reprise with an old lover. The affair was quickly discovered, despite their attempts at secrecy. The king reacted with self-pitying fury, especially when he learned that Catherine's numerous skills had been honed prior to marriage.

Catherine denied the allegations, but to no avail. The trial did not last long. Henry wept when he received her death warrant—but he signed it nonetheless. Catherine spent the night before her execution rehearsing how to place her head on the block. Presumably these efforts left her exhausted; her legs gave way as she climbed the scaffold and she had to be helped up.

Like a rose pruned prematurely, Catherine Howard was beheaded in 1542. She and Henry had been married less than two years.

CAUTIONARY MORAL
Don't mess around on the king.

Jane Grey

1554

ometimes survival is a matter of timing. Consider Lady Jane Grey—if she had been born just a decade later, she might not have been queen of England for only nine days. Instead of marching to the block at the tender age of sixteen, Jane could have hung out with Elizabeth I at court. Elizabeth would have championed the younger girl as they bonded over their dysfunctional families. They'd chat in Greek about philosophy, maybe even provide Shakespeare with a bon mot or two.

But this was not to be for Jane Grey. She was born too early and too closely related to the powers that be for a happy life.

Jane was the great-niece of Henry VIII and fourth in line to his throne, after Henry's three children. She was born in 1537 to a family greedy for power and scant on affection. Ever politically minded, her parents named her for Jane Seymour, the much-married king's then wife. Jane's mother considered the girl too sensitive, so she beat her regularly. This encouraged Jane to retreat into the life of the mind; she easily mastered several languages and was judged a brilliant scholar. At the age of nine, Jane's parents bundled her off to the home of Catherine Parr, Henry VIII's widowed queen, where the girl lived happily for the first time. Henry's daughter Elizabeth also inhabited this pleasant purgatory for inconvenient royals.

OUT OF THE MOUTHS OF BABES
The crown is not my right, and pleaseth me not.
The Lady Mary is the rightful heir.

Jane Grey

When Henry died in 1547, he was survived by his sixth wife, Catherine; a Catholic daughter, Mary; a Protestant daughter, Elizabeth; and his young son, Edward. King Edward VI was fond of his cousin Jane. They were the same age and similarly devoted to his father's new and improved Protestant religion. For these reasons and others, there was talk of marrying Jane to Edward, but it did not come to pass.

Edward also suffered from tuberculosis. Rapacious courtiers circled the boy king like vultures since upon his death the throne of England would be up for grabs—Henry's many marriages, annulments, and divorces left Edward's sisters' rights of succession as easily manipulated as Play-Doh.

One such courtier was John Dudley, the Duke of Northumberland. Dudley had been appointed by Henry VIII as one of the sixteen regents to guide Edward until he came of age; the duke used his position to seize as much influence as possible. Seeing that Edward was at death's door, Dudley mercilessly worked the king's hatred of Catholicism to convince him to leave the throne to Jane Grey, instead of Edward's next-in-line sibling Mary or the matrilineally compromised Elizabeth. To complete the coup, Dudley proposed that Jane's parents marry their daughter to his son, Guilford.

Poor Jane never had a chance. Against her will, her family eagerly agreed to all Dudley suggested. Jane's betrothal ceremony was preceded by a parental whipping to encourage her cooperation. Jane disliked her teenaged husband but feared her father-

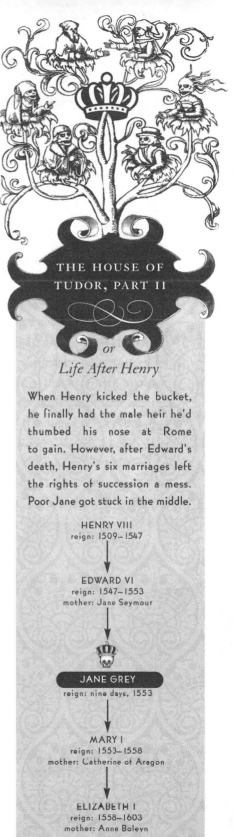

THE HOUSE OF TUDOR, PART II

or

Life After Henry

When Henry kicked the bucket, he finally had the male heir he'd thumbed his nose at Rome to gain. However, after Edward's death, Henry's six marriages left the rights of succession a mess. Poor Jane got stuck in the middle.

HENRY VIII
reign: 1509–1547

EDWARD VI
reign: 1547–1553
mother: Jane Seymour

JANE GREY
reign: nine days, 1553

MARY I
reign: 1553–1558
mother: Catherine of Aragon

ELIZABETH I
reign: 1558–1603
mother: Anne Boleyn

in-law—Guilford was vain and foolish, but Dudley was dangerous and cunning. Even though she was only fifteen, she understood she'd married into a family more treacherous than her own.

Soon after Jane's reluctant nuptials, Edward gasped his last breath. Jane wept and shook with fright at the news that she was to be queen. She refused the crown, but Dudley spun visions of tortured Protestant martyrs under Mary Tudor's Catholic rule. To protect the faith, Jane capitulated: "If what has been given to me is lawfully mine, may thy Divine Majesty grant me such spirit and grace that I may govern to thy glory and service. . . ."

Princess Mary did not take this snub lying down. While Dudley was in London haranguing Queen Jane to name Guilford king, Mary was off in the countryside raising an army. Nine days later, she had enough support to push Jane off her throne and into the Tower of London. Jane, Guilford, Dudley, and Jane's father were all sentenced to death. Initially, Mary planned to spare Jane and Guilford—she understood that the teenagers were only their parents' puppets. However, after further unrest, she realized that as long as they lived, the threats to her throne would continue.

Jane received the news of her execution calmly. "It was not my desire to prolong my days . . . I assure you, the time hath been so odious to me that I long for nothing so much as death." In other words, enough was enough.

Jane Grey was beheaded in 1554. For all of his sins, on one account Dudley was correct: Mary I executed several hundred Protestants during her reign, winning her the unwelcome nickname of Bloody Mary.

CAUTIONARY MORAL
Choose your in-laws carefully.

Mary signing Jane's death warrant.

Juana of Castile

1555

uana of Castile was the third daughter of Ferdinand, king of Aragon, and Isabella, queen of Castile; Juana's sister was Catherine of Aragon, who wound up divorced from Henry VIII. Though Ferdinand and Isabella gained fame by bankrolling the explorer Columbus, Juana's obsessive love for her husband gained her a different sort of fame. Her sedate childhood did not reveal the passionate nature that would one day win her the nickname of Juana the Mad. Today a psychiatrist would simply call her bipolar and throw a handful of lithium at her.

Born in 1479, Juana was groomed from an early age to marry and expand her parents' influence. She did not protest when her parents sent her off at sixteen to wed Philip the Handsome, the Duke of Burgundy. Turns out that Philip's nickname was accurate—and Juana fell madly, irrevocably in love with him at first sight. The couple begged to marry the night of their first meeting, so they could consummate their union without delay.

Life with Juana and Philip was a fun house of sex and fighting. Though Philip was delighted that his wife was hot in the sack, he was threatened by her loyalty to all things Spanish—especially her parents' politics. Juana did not like the way her husband bossed her around, and she threw tantrums over his fondness for other women. One unfortunate lady-in-waiting had her long hair personally shorn by Juana after she discovered Philip servicing her; Juana deposited the tresses on her husband's pillow as a friendly warning. She also indulged in love potions and spells.

Despite the drama, Juana did not neglect her royal duties and gave birth to five children in rapid succession. Real life intervened when Juana's mother passed away in 1504, leaving Juana queen of Castile. Juana's father,

Ferdinand, attempted to use her wild behavior as an excuse to grab Castile from her. Though Queen Juana protested, it was soon moot: Philip suddenly succumbed to illness in 1506 at twenty-eight, leaving her without an ally. On top of this, she was pregnant yet again with a sixth child.

All of these events pushed the queen's sanity to the breaking point: Juana became unhinged with grief. She embraced Philip's corpse as if he still lived. Though heavy with child, she accompanied his coffin to its final resting place in Granada, insisting they travel at night so women would not be tempted by him. Occasionally, she'd open the coffin to greet his remains. During these travels, Juana gave birth to a daughter, whom she named after her sister queen in England.

No surprise here: Ferdinand milked Juana's behavior for all it was worth—countries were worth more than daughters. He declared Juana insane and locked her away in a chamber in the castle of Tordesillas. She was to stay there for the rest of her life.

After Ferdinand died, Juana's son Charles took over her throne. She received no mercy from him either. He wrote to her caretaker, "It seems to me that the best and most suitable thing for you to do is to make sure that no person speaks with Her Majesty, for no good could come of it."

Juana died in 1555 at seventy-five, after almost fifty years of imprisonment.

CAUTIONARY MORAL
You can't reason with insanity.

Insanity

In the unstable world of the ruling class, consolidating power was the best way to protect your throne from wannabes. The easiest way to do so? Keep it in the family!

This wisdom led to massive consanguinity within royal families. In ancient Egypt, brother married sister, sanctioned by the example of goddess Isis and her brother-husband, Osiris. However, in Europe getting cozy with your sibling was verboten. Nonetheless, nieces married uncles with alacrity, as did first cousins. And anyone who's read an H. C. Lovecraft horror story knows that inbreeding leads to a host of genetic problems, including mental instability.

Was Juana really mad or just lovelorn? She was a member of the Spanish Hapsburg dynasty, which specialized in producing inbred and insane monarchs. Juana's great-great-great grandson Carlos II was called "the Bewitched" due to his obvious mental deficiencies, which were blamed on evil spirits. Carlos spent his less than illustrious reign presiding over the Spanish Inquisition's largest auto-da-fé. He unsuccessfully attempted to have children with the lovely Marie Luisa of Orléans, who died under mysterious circumstances— but that's another story.

Jeanne III of Navarre

1572

ike most princesses of small, powerless countries, Jeanne of Navarre was born to be wed. Navarre was a border kingdom trapped between the mighty Catholic powers of France and Spain, and it served as refuge for French Calvinists, or Huguenots. Jeanne's father wasted no time in shipping the girl off at thirteen to marry William, Duke of Cleves. However, unlike other princesses, Jeanne did not suffer in silence. She wrote, "I, Jehanne de Navarre, continuing my protests already made, in which I persist, say and declare and protest again by these present that the marriage proposed between me and the Duke of Cleves is against my will, that I have never consented to it. . . . I do not know to whom to appeal except to God."

Apparently Jeanne's prayers were effective: Four years later her marriage was annulled. The vindicated princess did not forget God's help, even when she was next wed to Antoine de Bourbon, a prince of France. Initially this was a happier match. It produced five children, the first of whom was an heir, Henri. The couple lived peacefully until her father's death in 1555, which made them corulers of Navarre.

Now queen, Jeanne found a new way to express her gratitude to God— she converted to Calvinism and declared it the

Jeanne III. A poisoned peacemaker?

official religion of Navarre. Antoine accepted his wife's faith, but he was swayed back to Catholicism when the Spanish king dangled Sardinia as a bribe for religious compliance. The couple separated but continued to antagonize each other. In 1562, Antoine was killed in the French Religious Wars which, not surprisingly, sprang up between Catholics and Huguenots.

With her husband out of the way, Queen Jeanne gained a new political and religious adversary. Catherine de' Medici ruled Catholic France as regent for her son Charles IX, who was mentally unstable; the rest of her sons weren't so hot either. Catherine was well aware that if her sons died without issue, Jeanne's little son Henri would inherit the throne of France, thus bringing the horrors of Calvinism home. Catherine even consulted her favorite necromancer, Nostradamus, who predicted that Henri would become king. Superstitious Catherine decided to fight fate and was willing to plot, murder, or poison to do so. At the start of the war, she was accused of giving a perfumed apple to one of Jeanne's allies; his dog dropped dead after tasting it. She also attempted to have Jeanne assassinated.

Since poison and murder did not work, Catherine fell back on diplomacy: She proposed Jeanne marry Henri to her daughter. Jeanne was dubious: "A peace made of snow this winter . . . would melt in next summer's heat." Nonetheless, she reluctantly agreed after the French queen promised to practice religious tolerance to end the war.

Jeanne died in Paris under suspicious circumstances two months before Henri's marriage in 1572. Though an autopsy concluded the forty-four-year-old queen had tuberculosis, rumors flew that Catherine had given her a pair of poisoned gloves, perhaps to wear to her son's wedding.

CAUTIONARY MORAL
*If it seems too good to be true,
it probably is.*

*Catherine as a
not so sweet young thing.*

Mary Stuart

1587

ary Stuart, better known as Mary, Queen of Scots, was born with two strikes against her, both of which would doom her to an early grave.

The first strike was her cousin Elizabeth, who ruled over England after many years of blood-filled religious strife. Elizabeth was Protestant. Mary was a devout Catholic—and this was the second strike. Mary's religion made the Scottish queen a seductive alternative for those who yearned for a Catholic monarch. Elizabeth was understandably skittish around her cousin and kept her at arm's length.

Mary's life was as colorful as it was tragic. The only daughter of King James V of Scotland, she was born in 1542 on a December day sacred to the Virgin Mary. Some took this as a good omen, but her father did not. He died a week after her birth, leaving Mary to rule Scotland from her crib. She was crowned queen before her first birthday.

The little queen's reign was tumultuous from the start. Mary's neighbor to the south, the much-married Henry VIII of England, planned to wed his son, Edward, to Mary to join their two nations. He used military force to press his suit. When the king's army came too close to the Scottish border for comfort, Mary was sent to France at the age of five. It was here that she became a sixteenth-century case study of Women Who Love Too Much.

Mary was famed for her beauty, intelligence, and kindness. Henri II, the king of France, considered her the most charming child he had ever seen and betrothed her to his son, the four-year-old dauphin François, thus consolidating Scotland and France as a power. The two royal children were raised together in France and grew fond of each other. They were wed in 1558, when Mary was fifteen.

OUT OF THE MOUTHS OF BABES
No more tears now; I will think upon revenge.

Mary Stuart

But marital happiness proved elusive. Upon Henry II's death in 1559, Mary and François were crowned king and queen of France. Less than a year later, François died of an ear infection. Heartbroken, Mary unwisely decided to return to Scotland, though it was still deemed dangerous.

During Mary's ten-year sojourn in France, Henry VIII had succumbed to death and the throne of England had seen several uneasy occupants of varying religious loyalties. At last Mary's Protestant cousin Elizabeth reigned—and there was no way the queen of England was going to be usurped by the queen of Scotland.

To protect herself, Mary Stuart wed Henry Stewart, Lord Darnley. Though Darnley was Catholic and English, the marriage did not bring her peace—but it did make them next in line to Elizabeth's throne, a choice that irked the English monarch. Darnley bullied Mary to make him more than her consort. He grew jealous of Mary's friendship with her secretary and arranged for his murder while she was six months pregnant. Not long after the birth of their son, James, Darnley was found strangled in his garden.

Some thought Mary was involved in the murder, but others blamed it on James Hepburn, the Protestant Earl of Bothwell. Soon after Darnley's death, Bothwell kidnapped Mary with the aid of a small army of eight hundred men. Their inevitable marriage, which was

Mary and Darnley before marital discontent kicked in.

cemented by Protestant vows, created even more unrest in Scotland. Hoping for Elizabeth's sympathy, Mary fled to England in 1568, abandoning sweet baby James to be raised by Protestant Scottish nobles. Instead, Elizabeth imprisoned Mary. Elizabeth wavered for nineteen years before she finally ordered her cousin's death by beheading. Mary was only forty-four years old and had spent almost half her life in prison.

A queen to the end, Mary played the drama to the hilt. She adorned herself in a regal black gown over a red chemise—the color of martyrdom in the Catholic Church. This red chemise was revealed to a shocked audience when the executioners undressed the monarch of her gown and petticoats for the chopping block. Mary quipped, "Never have I put off my clothes before such a company."

It took three ax blows to sever Mary's head from her neck. After the first one, she was heard to murmur *"mon dieu"*—my god. Elizabeth immediately ordered all her cousin's possessions burned to prevent anyone hoarding them as religious relics.

CAUTIONARY MORAL
Respect your cousin in the family business.

LIFE AFTER DEATH

Mary had the last laugh. To preserve her power, Elizabeth remained unmarried and without issue. Her closest relative was Mary's son, James, who became king of Scotland at the age of one. Upon Elizabeth's death in 1603, James inherited the crown of England, uniting the two countries in Protestant glory. Some believe that James's unpopular policies eventually led to the English Civil War faced by his son, Charles I. So much for Elizabeth's golden age!

King of it all.

Mumtaz Mahal

1631

here's an old saying that if you love someone, set them free; if they truly love you, they will return. In the case of India's Mumtaz Mahal, it was death that freed her from the loving embrace of her husband, the Mughal emperor Shah Jahan I. Since Mumtaz was unable to return to him for obvious reasons—corpses aren't able to do much beyond rotting in a grave—Shah Jahan used his sorrow to memorialize her with the most fabulous tomb ever.

Little is known about Mumtaz outside of the romantic devotion she inspired in Shah Jahan. One fact is certain: Mumtaz was originally named Arjumand Banu Begum upon her birth in 1593. Shah Jahan granted her the title of Mumtaz Mahal— Persian for "chosen one of the palace"—after their 1612 wedding. Since polygamy was de rigueur for a ruler, the monarch had several other wives. But they were accorded scant attention—Mumtaz was far and away Shah Jahan's favorite. Court historians of the era recorded the steaming intensity of the couple's erotic connection, which was noteworthy even to a culture ripened on the teachings of the *Kama Sutra*.

Thirteen children followed in the wake of their hot passion. However, a fourteenth proved unlucky—Mumtaz did not survive the birth of a daughter in 1631. She was thirty-nine and had been married to the shah for nineteen years. The emperor was inconsolable. Though he outlived his wife by thirty-four years, he never embraced another woman.

One story claims that Mumtaz's dying wish was for Shah Jahan to build a monument to their enduring love. A cynic cannot help but wonder if this was a rumor bandied about by the emperor to deflect criticism from the cost of assuaging his loss—the Taj Mahal cost more than 32 million rupees, perhaps the most expensive grief therapy session known to humanity.

Mumtaz's corpse rests there still today, a testament to eternal love and sublime architecture.

CAUTIONARY MORAL
Love can't bring the dead back to life,
but it can inspire great art.

A BRIEF DIGRESSION
It took more than fifteen years and a large team of architects to build the Taj Mahal, one of the seven wonders of the modern world. It is located near a garden favored by Mumtaz. Rumors that Shah Jahan executed craftsmen who displeased him during the mausoleum's construction remain unsubstantiated.

End-of-Chapter Quiz
or
What We Have Learned So Far

1. What was the legacy of Henry VIII's multimarrying ways?

○ a. The acceptance of workplace romances.

○ b. A Tammy Wynette song entitled "D-I-V-O-R-C-E."

○ c. Neck ruffs—great for deflecting the executioner's ax.

○ d. A spanking brand-new church for religious martyrs to rally around.

Neck ruff: fashion statement or lifesaver?

2. What did Jane Grey and Jeanne of Navarre have in common?

○ a. Both believed the Catholic Church was not the true faith.

○ b. Both had supportive parents.

○ c. Both reigned only nine days.

○ d. Both claimed to be BFF with Catherine de' Medici.

3. Why didn't Mary Stuart and Elizabeth I get along?

○ a. Because they were cousins in the family business.

○ b. Religious differences.

○ c. They disagreed over Shakespeare's use of iambic pentameter.

○ d. Elizabeth suspected Mary was measuring for drapes in the throne room.

4. Why was Juana of Castile insane?

○ a. The travails of inbreeding.

○ b. Her husband made her hot and bothered.

○ c. The emotional stress of widowhood.

○ d. Her father was conniving and selfish.

5. Which statement is true about Mumtaz Mahal?

○ a. Her husband thought she was the bee's knees.

○ b. She was named Mumtaz Mahal by her parents.

○ c. She couldn't get knocked up to save her life.

○ d. She designed the Taj Mahal after her death.

CHAPTER FIVE

Go Baroque

OUT OF THE MOUTHS OF BABES

I was a queen, and you took away my crown;
a wife, and you killed my husband; a mother, and
you deprived me of my children; my blood alone
remains; take it, but do not make me suffer long.

Marie Antoinette

The beheadings espoused by Henry VIII and cohorts were eventually replaced by a more sinister force: the philosophy of Jean-Jacques Rousseau. Rousseau was born in Switzerland in 1712, over a century after Mary Stuart revealed her red chemise to a stunned executioner. He wrote prolifically enough that folks of the era could project whatever they wanted onto his words. The philosopher's widely read publications included a romantic novel (*Julie, or the New Héloïse*); an autobiography (*Confessions*); and, most troublesome of all for royal necks, philosophical discourses presenting the radical concept that the sovereignty of the state rested on the will of the people. Napoléon allegedly said of Rousseau, "It would have been better for the peace of France if this man had never existed."

In France, both Robespierre, a leader of the French Revolution, and Marie Antoinette, the wife of King Louis XVI, were swooning to Jean-Jacques—but for different reasons. Marie Antoinette found the philosopher's romanticization of nature a relief from the artifice of royal life. The queen attempted to embody Rousseauesque ideals by building a play village, the *petit hameau*, where she and her friends could live the rustic life. As for Robespierre, he interpreted Rousseau's famous words "Man was born free, and everywhere he is in chains" as an invitation to kill the royals. Up in Denmark, Rousseau's writings prompted the lover of Queen Caroline Matilda to revamp the government, leading to her dethronement.

This turbulent era was capped by the murder of Marie Antoinette by the peasants she had aped at the *petit hameau*. The queen's execution elevated the guillotine from personal threat into fashion statement. Upper-crust ladies adorned their earlobes and necks with jewelry sporting tiny guillotines or tied red ribbons around their throats. Not wanting to be left out of the fun, men cropped their hair *à la victime*.

Even though Madame la Guillotine dominated these Grand Guignol–inspiring times, the prosaic reality was that royal women were still just as likely to be felled by suspicious illnesses, defects of inbreeding, imprisonment, or starvation. And, as ever, beware of childbirth.

Margarita Theresa of Spain

1673

hough a picture captures a moment in time, the story it tells is often unclear. One example: Velázquez's painting *Las Meninas* is considered one of the greatest works of Western art. Yet its intentions are still debated four hundred years later. Is it an informal portrait of the Spanish royal family? A snide commentary on court life? Or a meditation on the act of observation? These theories reflect as much about the viewer as they do the artist. Regardless, one truth cannot be denied: The composition of *Las Meninas* centers around an unusually self-possessed five-year-old princess, Margarita Theresa of Spain.

Upon viewing this lustrous, golden portrait of Margarita it is hard to imagine that her future would offer anything but years of privilege and felicity. The reality was quite different. Margarita was never to grow old, never to see her beauty dim—she died at the age of twenty-one. It was a sad ending for the favorite child of Philip IV of Spain; in his letters, the king addressed the princess as "my joy."

Born in 1651, Margarita Theresa was the first offspring of the king and his second wife, Mariana of Austria; Mariana was Philip's niece and almost thirty years his junior. Margarita entered the world improbably untouched by the effects of inbreeding, though her future siblings would not be so fortunate. Nonetheless, the princess was promised in marriage while still a child to the Holy Roman Emperor Leopold I, which was an even more incestuous coupling than her parents'. Leopold just happened to be Margarita's maternal uncle and paternal first cousin. On the plus side, he was only eleven years older than she.

The couple did not meet until their wedding, when Margarita was a mature fifteen-year-old and Leopold a youthful twenty-six. Luckily, the hot flames of regard had been stoked by Velázquez, who had painted several portraits of the Spanish princess besides *Las Meninas* in his capacity as court artist. These paintings had been sent from Madrid to the Holy Roman Emperor's palace in Vienna, enabling Leopold to observe his future empress from afar as she matured.

Despite the gap in their ages, Margarita and Leopold were very happy together. They shared a love of the arts and appear to have been compatible, an unusual situation for dynastic marriages. Four offspring rapidly followed their union—and led to the empress's premature end. Of these children, only a daughter named Maria Antonia survived to reach adulthood; the other three died in infancy.

CAUTIONARY MORAL
Though a picture tells a story,
it may not reveal the truth.

A BRIEF DIGRESSION

Diego Velázquez painted *Las Meninas* in 1656. Its title refers to the maids waiting on Margarita Theresa in the oil painting; they include a dwarf, who is hardly taller than the magnificently attired young princess. Velázquez included a self-portrait on the left of the main composition. The baroque painter Luca Giordano praised *Las Meninas* as the "theology of painting."

Maria Luisa of Orléans

1689

 he calamitous fertility of Queen Margarita Theresa stands in marked contrast to her younger brother, Carlos II. Though both siblings were born of the same parents, the consequences of inbreeding flowered fully in Carlos. His head and jaw were seriously misshapen, forcing him to subsist on the milk of fourteen wet nurses until he was five years old, when it is assumed he learned how to feed himself. He had to be carried like a baby for much of his childhood and did not walk until nearly grown. Worst of all, his mental faculties were those of an imbecile. Nonetheless, Carlos inherited the throne of Spain at the age of four after the death of his father, Philip IV, in 1665. Though incapable of ruling without his mother's guidance, he was still expected to procreate—which might have been possible if the king's equipment hadn't followed suit with the rest of his sorry self.

Who knows what Louis XIV, France's famed Sun King, was thinking when he arranged for his lovely, vivacious niece Maria Luisa of Orléans to wed the deformed Carlos—clearly he was considering the political advantages over her personal happiness. Louis presented the match as a fait accompli to the princess, stating he could not have done more for his own daughter. "But you could have done more for your niece!" Maria Luisa allegedly protested.

Maria Luisa. Beautiful but . . .

129

In spite of the princess's lack of enthusiasm, the betrothal moved forward. The negotiations were encouraged by Carlos himself, who decided that he was madly in love after viewing his fiancée's fetching portrait.

Carlos and Maria Luisa's 1679 wedding festivities culminated with an auto-da-fé in which over a hundred supposed heretics were either judged or executed, presumably to curry God's favor for a fruitful union. It did not work—though the marriage was consummated, Maria Luisa's womb remained resolutely empty. Undeterred, the royal couple continued to petition the heavens for a child. A contemporary wrote that they prayed "with such faith that even the stones would move in order to join them and ask God for the issue they desire."

Between the pressures of infertility and the oppressive Spanish court, Maria Luisa sank into depression and obesity. Death suddenly overtook her at the age of twenty-seven, after two days of excruciating stomach pain. Most likely she had appendicitis, but some suspected she was poisoned by her mother-in-law, who might have decided that another queen would be more successful at coaxing heirs from her son. Maria Luisa's last words were, "Your Majesty might have other wives, but no one will love you as I do."

Carlos was distraught at his queen's unexpected death—as simple as he was, he really did adore her. Following in the familial footsteps of his great-great-great grandmother Juana of Castile, he insisted on opening the coffin to visit his spouse's remains. Carlos was not allowed to mourn for long; within six months he was wed to a new bride, who also (surprise, surprise) did not conceive. The king concluded that there could be only one cause for his maladies: witchcraft.

Carlos consulted an exorcist in 1698. His learned judgment? The king was bewitched by an enchanted cup of bedtime chocolate given to him as a boy by his mother. Though the appropriate rites were observed, Carlos's condition only worsened—after all, exorcisms can't halt the genetic ravages of inbreeding. The king's mortal misery came to an end two years later.

Because Carlos was the last of his line, his succession was settled in a manner that must have pleased Maria Luisa's uncle. The Spanish crown passed to the Sun King's French grandson, Philippe of Anjou.

CAUTIONARY MORAL
The soil is only as good as the seed.

Sophia Alekseyevna

1704

s the daughter of the tsar, Sophia Alekseyevna was des-
tined for an isolated, barren existence. The tsarevna's
exalted rank forbade her from marrying below herself,
so no man could make her a wife and mother. Her status also precluded her from leaving her luxurious private quarters unless she was shielded from onlookers by
a curtain of red silk. By all accounts, Sophia should have had a soporific life
where only her birth and death earned notice—but she was no ordinary
Russian woman. Instead, the tsarevna used her tremendous intelligence and
ambition to become the first woman to rule Russia.

Born in 1657, Sophia was the only surviving daughter
of Tsar Alexei I by his first wife, Maria. She was also
the half sister of Peter the Great, her father's son
by his second wife, Natalya. Sophia had
one advantage that most other Russian
women didn't: a world-class education.
Somehow the tsarevna had convinced
her father to let her share lessons with
Fyodor, her sickly heir-to-the-throne
brother; the educations of her two
younger brothers, Ivan and Peter, were
ignored, since it was presumed they
were too far down the line of succession to ever become tsar.

Sophia's brilliance won notice. The
monk scholar Simeon Polotsky observed
that Sophia possessed an "accomplished masculine

Peter wearing armor. He needed it.

mind"—high praise indeed. To gain power, Sophia rebelled in small but significant ways within her conscribed world. She attended council meetings, where she was introduced to the boyars, nobles who influenced Russian policy. When Fyodor inherited the throne after their father's death in 1676, she became her brother's main confidante.

Fyodor wasn't long for the world—he died in 1682 at the age of twenty. Ten-year-old Peter was chosen tsar over Ivan since Ivan was an invalid, like Fyodor, and blind to boot. But wily Sophia spread rumors that Peter's relatives had poisoned Fyodor, inciting the army to violence. Sophia used the opportunity to grab the throne, claiming she'd rule on behalf of both Ivan and Peter until they grew old enough to reign jointly.

Sophia was a happy regent until Peter turned seventeen in 1689. After much Sturm und Drang, she surrendered the throne and sought sanctuary in a convent. But support for Sophia simmered during the new tsar's reign. A decade later, when Peter was absent from the country, sympathizers attempted to reinstate her. The uprising was quickly squashed. As a warning, the rebels' corpses were hung in front of Sophia's windows.

Sophia got the hint. To protect herself, she donned the habit. This time, there was no retreating from becoming the bride of Christ, the only spouse worthy of the tsarevna. Sophia spent the remainder of her life in solitary confinement.

CAUTIONARY MORAL
The best candidate doesn't always get the job.

THE HOUSE OF ROMANOV

or
When Peter Isn't So Great

Peter's road to tsardom was filled with danger, partially due to his too-clever-by-half half sister, Sophia. He retaliated by pushing her into joining a religious order.

ALEXIS I
reign: 1645–1676

FYODOR III
reign: 1676–1682

SOPHIA
Alekseyevna
reign: 1682–1689

PETER I —— **IVAN V**
coreign: 1682–1696

PETER I
the Great
reign: 1682–1725

Mangammal

1704

n the antebellum novel *Gone with the Wind*, Rhett Butler tells a swathed-in-black-crepe Scarlett O'Hara, "Personally, I think suttee much more merciful than our charming Southern custom of burying widows alive." One woman besides Scarlett who disagreed with Rhett was Mangammal—but then, she was a rara avis who refused to commit suttee after the death of her husband, Chokkanatha Nayak, ruler of the south Indian kingdom of Madurai Nayak. Instead, she did the unthinkable for a widow of her seventeenth-century milieu: She tried on his crown and found it fit just right.

Mangammal was born within the penumbra of power. Her father was a general in Chokkanatha's army; presumably the king thought highly enough of him that he chose Mangammal for one of his wives. Upon Chokkanatha's death in 1682, their son ascended the throne—but not for long. He joined his father in the grave in 1689, leaving an infant son as his only heir; his widow chose suttee over single motherhood.

With no one else available to rule, Mangammal became queen regent for her grandson, with the

A BRIEF DIGRESSION Suttee, or sati, is a funeral ritual in which a Hindu widow commits suicide by sacrificing herself on her husband's funeral pyre. Translated literally, the word *sati* means "virtuous woman." By choosing to join her spouse in death, the widow purged their sins and elevated herself into a deity; *suttee* is a nineteenth-century English phonetic spelling of *sati*.

Though suttee was primarily practiced by higher-caste women (such as those from the warrior or priestly classes), it was also a tradition with ancient Greeks, Egyptians, and Scandinavians. Though abolished in 1829, suttee still rears its controversial head. In 1987, eighteen-year-old widow Roop Kanwar adorned herself in her wedding finery and willingly chose a fiery death.

understanding that she would hand over the crown when he reached maturity. It is here that Mangammal stepped up to the plate and, much to her subjects' surprise, hit a home run out of the park. Initially Madurai was resistant to the idea of a female monarch, but the queen ruled with such acumen that she won much popularity. To improve the infrastructure of her land, she built many roads and temples, one of which serves today as the Gandhi Museum. Many towns were named after her, in acknowledgment of her good works. She also proved to be a capable commander in chief during wartime.

But this golden age could not last. When Mangammal's grandson came of age in 1704, she refused to abdicate. After all, she had done such a stellar job—why should she pass power to one less capable, even if he was her own flesh and blood?

In the end, the queen's flesh was destroyed by its need for sustenance instead of by flames. Mangammal's grandson and his generals arranged for her to be locked in the palace prison, never to be seen again. Most accounts claim that she starved to death while in captivity.

CAUTIONARY MORAL
*Knowing when to surrender
can save your life.*

Starvation

It must have been apparent to humans early on that lack of food equals lack of life—starvation has been used for executions since the dawn of civilization. It was especially favored in the Graeco-Roman world among the high and mighty, who saw it as a discreet way to rid themselves of a troublesome relative or a vestal not so virgin. As in Mangammal's case, political disagreements were easily settled by simply locking someone up and throwing away the key. No messy public trials or executions—just a body to dispose of quietly in the dead of night.

The poet Dante described one such death in his *Inferno*. Count Ugolino was imprisoned with his offspring for betraying the city of Pisa. To ease his hunger, his sons offered their flesh: "Father, much less pain 'twill give us / If thou do eat of us; thyself didst clothe us / With this poor flesh, and do thou strip it off." Ugolino's acceptance of their generous offer earned him a special place in Dante's hell.

None for you, your majesty.

Caroline Matilda

1775

aroline Matilda was the youngest sister of George III of England; their father had died several months before her birth in 1751, leaving him in charge of raising her. When Caroline reached the fecund age of sixteen, King George trundled her off to become queen of Denmark. Unfortunately no one bothered to warn her that there was something rotten in Denmark—her fiancé, Christian VII.

From his earliest childhood, there was something weird about Christian. While other kids were playing with toys, Christian stared catatonically at his hands. Obsessed with having a perfect body, he unbuttoned his shirt in public to check his six-pack. The king became stranger as he grew older. He liked to pretend that he was a criminal in need of corporal punishment; other times, he wore disguises in public, where he picked brawls and indulged in kinky sex with prostitutes. In his darker moments, Christian babbled nonsense and shouted about killing himself and others.

In other words, Christian was stark raving mad. All this wouldn't have been so bad, except he did not want to be king of Denmark.

Enter Caroline. Predictably, she was appalled at the dismal marriage her brother had arranged for her. But instead of running home to England—she was too furious for that—she embraced Denmark as its regent. King Christian did not mind her taking over. Instead, he liked it—it fueled his fantasies of female domination, a fact not lost on his dismayed courtiers.

Thoughout all this, Queen Caroline did not neglect her royal duty. She managed to conceive an heir of Christian, Frederick, who was born in 1768. After this, Christian considered his job done and the queen was left to follow her own pleasures as she wished. Which she did—Caroline developed a crush on Christian's doctor, Johann Friedrich Struensee, that she quickly consummated. Their passionate affair became an open secret that the king either didn't notice or care two hoots about. Nor did he blink when Caroline gave birth to an illegitimate daughter, whom she claimed was his.

The Danish lovebirds could have continued singing indefinitely, but Struensee got all Rousseauesque on Caroline. The good doctor fancied himself a philosopher humanist. With the king incapacitated, Struensee used his position with the queen to push some of his more radical ideas into law and name himself de facto head of state.

The Danish people were not amused. A plot was launched in 1772 to overthrow Caroline and Struensee's rule, headed by Christian's dowager stepmother, Juliana Marie. The conspirators used the pageantry of a masquerade ball to conceal their plans. Caroline was too distracted by wine and song to notice what was going on until it was too late—she and Struensee were arrested that night, never to see each other again.

Caroline was imprisoned in a castle at Elsinore, where another mad Dane reputedly lived. Her children were taken away from her and her marriage to Christian dissolved. Struensee's fate was far less kind. He was convicted of treason and ultimately drawn and quartered.

Eventually Caroline was released from prison. Instead of going home to England, she settled in Celle, Germany. There she plotted her return to Denmark to regain her throne and her children. Alas, all her plans were brought to a close after she succumbed to scarlet fever in 1775. Too bad there wasn't a doctor in the house.

CAUTIONARY MORAL
Don't look to your doctor to heal your disappointments.

Marie Antoinette

1793

irst things first: Marie Antoinette never said, "Let them eat cake." Those words were attributed to an earlier French queen, Marie-Thérèse, the wife of Sun King Louis XIV. By 1767—a year in which Marie Antoinette was still an innocent German-speaking twelve-year-old in Austria—this quote had been bandied about enough that the philosopher Rousseau included it in his *Confessions*: "I recollected the thoughtless saying of a great princess, who, on being informed that the country people had no bread, replied, 'Then let them eat pastry!'"

But these facts did not dissuade *citoyens* of eighteenth-century France from inflating "let them eat cake" into a poisoned soufflé to shove down Marie Antoinette's diamond-adorned throat. The truth is that, in times of turmoil, people look for a scapegoat to sacrifice. Marie Antoinette just happened to be the French Revolution's favorite It girl.

To be fair, Marie Antoinette lived in a world in which she was expected to obey her husband as if he were God, to spill forth children as if she were Eve—and to accept that aristocrats ate cake while peasants had no bread. After all, it was divine will and all that.

Marie was born to be oblivious in 1755. She was the fifteenth child of the Austrian empress Maria Theresa, who raised the

Marie in better days.

pretty little archduchess to be a tasty linzer torte on the pastry shelf of European princesses. The empress did not let her linger past her expiration date. She married off Marie two months after her first menstruation in 1770 to Louis-Auguste, the future king of France. She was only fourteen.

Marie did her best to adapt to the sophisticated French court, but she was ill prepared. Originally an older sister was intended as Louis's queen and had been educated accordingly; an outbreak of smallpox bumped her from Maria Theresa's dynastic lineup. Instead, the empress beefed up Marie's lackluster studies to include French history and informed the girl to go forth and procreate for France: "If one is to consider only the greatness of your position, you are the happiest of your sisters and all princesses."

But happiness was elusive for Marie, though she did her best to win her husband's favor. Louis-Auguste may have been next in line to the throne, but he was a porcine-visaged geek who preferred hunting and carpentry to romancing the fair sex. Their marriage remained unconsummated for seven years, during which time Marie endured malicious gossip at court, an unattentive husband, and monthly letters from her mother nagging her about her maidenhead. Marie wept as she saw other ladies of the court grow big with child. Upon hearing that one had suffered a stillbirth, she confessed, "Even though it is terrible, I still wish it had been me in her place."

The problem, however, lay with Louis, not Marie—and no amount of Viagra would have helped. Louis suffered from phimosis, a deformation of the foreskin that made sex excruciating for him. The only cure was circumcision, a dangerous operation in an age lacking anesthesia and antibiotics.

To distract herself from bed, birthing, and beyond, Marie frenetically indulged in retail therapy. Feathers, gowns, coiffures, and diamonds became her favored objects of desire. She stayed up all night gambling, racking up the royal debt in the process. When the pleasures of materialism proved ineffective, she turned to the consolation of philosophy. A reading of that old scamp Rousseau convinced Marie that salvation lay in nature. She planted gardens and built the *petit hameau*, a faux village on the grounds of Versailles, where she and her friends could play out their rustic fantasies.

Marie's activities did not go unnoticed by the people of France. While she was rhapsodizing over strawberries and goat milk at the *petit hameau*, the third estate was being taxed to starvation to pay for her luxuries. On top of this, bad weather left the poor without wheat for bread. When their com-

Guillotine

The formal history of the guillotine began in 1789 when a Dr. Joseph-Ignace Guillotin submitted a modest proposal to an assembly evaluating changes to the French penal code. Within it, Guillotin made the audacious suggestion that all men be treated equal when executed—that is, without pain and without torture. He wrote, "In all cases where the law imposes the death penalty on an accused person, the punishment shall be the same. . . . The criminal shall be decapitated; this will be done solely by means of a simple mechanism."

After nearly two years of debate, the Assembly approved his measure in time for the Reign of Terror's communal bloodletting. Previously, only nobility were beheaded; the hoi polloi met their

Les sans-culottes!

plaints went unheeded by the powers that be, they used the power of the press to point fingers. Marie—aka Madame Deficit or *l'Autrichienne* (the Austrian bitch)—was their favorite object of scorn. They circulated pornographic caricatures of her servicing women and men. It mattered little when Marie tried to reform her ways or that she was sympathetic to the poor in her private life.

It was during this period in 1774 that Louis's father unexpectedly died, thrusting the couple onto the throne. Louis XVI was as reluctant to govern as he was to make love, and the nation edged into bankruptcy. However, it seems that he gathered the courage to undergo the necessary surgery to impregnate Marie, for the queen was overjoyed to finally provide the people of France with an heir in 1781. Though other children followed, her oldest son died and a daughter did not survive infancy. But the private sorrows of royalty mattered little as the nation succumbed to chaos.

The storming of the Bastille, a prison housing political prisoners and a handy supply of firearms, signaled the start of the French Revolution on July 14, 1789. Two months later, a mob marched on Versailles to protest the lack of bread. The royal family was taken by force to the Tuileries in Paris, where they became prisoners in all but name. They disguised themselves as servants and attempted to escape, but were captured when the king was identified from coins bearing his profile.

This desperate act was viewed by the revolutionary forces as an act of treason—but the truth was that no matter what Marie and Louis did, the monarchy was doomed. Marie resigned herself to "remain passive and prepare to die." The king and queen were stripped of their royal titles and moved to a more secure prison to await judgment.

Louis was the first victim to lose his head in January 1793. Marie's hair supposedly turned white overnight from fear. Ten months later, after separation from her children and a sham trial for crimes against the state that included the molestation of her son, the queen formerly known as Madame Deficit sacrificed her life to Madame la Guillotine for the good of France. In an ideal world, wheat would have sprouted from her blood to feed the masses. *Vive la république!*

CAUTIONARY MORAL
When you play at being a peasant,
you risk being killed by one.

maker by more painful means, such as hanging or torture.

Contrary to popular belief, Guillotin was not a fetishist fascinated by executions; he was a lapsed Jesuit who hoped that a more humane method would lead to the abolition of the death penalty. Nor did he design the "simple mechanism" that bore his name. Variations of this egalitarian death bringer were recorded from the fourteenth century.

Did the guillotine really render its victims a painless, swift death? The jury is out on that, since no one can tell us. However, one story suggests that consciousness did not immediately cease after the blade fell. Charlotte Corday, the infamous murderess of Marat, was recorded to have blushed with "unequivocal indignation" after her severed head was slapped by her jubilant executioner.

Fortunately for those who value their heads, the guillotine was retired from public service in France in 1977.

Adieu, cruel world.

End-of-Chapter Quiz
or
What We Have Learned So Far

1. Rousseau's writings encouraged people to:

◯ a. Embrace nature like an expensive courtesan.

◯ b. Throw off their royal oppressors.

◯ c. Sharpen the blade of the guillotine.

◯ d. Go ahead—pursue that dream of *liberté, égalité, fraternité*, or bust.

2. What was the matter with Maria Luisa's hubby, Carlos?

◯ a. He was bewitched as a child.

◯ b. He did not have a big enough auto-da-fé.

◯ c. He had severe genetic defects from inbreeding.

◯ d. Not enough breast-feeding.

*Rousseau:
troublemaker
extraordinaire?*

3. Sophia Alekseyevna was expected since her birth to:

◯ a. Be seen and not heard.

◯ b. Be heard and not seen.

◯ c. Not be seen or heard.

◯ d. Herd animals on stage for the mise-en-scène.

4. Why didn't Mangammal commit suttee?

◯ a. She had a grandson to raise and a country to run.

◯ b. She was allergic to fire.

◯ c. She received a dispensation from the pope.

◯ d. There was a shortage of kindling that season.

5. Which quote really belongs to Marie Antoinette?

◯ a. "Man was born free, and everywhere he is in chains."

◯ b. "A queen who is not regent ought, under these circumstances, to remain passive and prepare to die."

◯ c. "Then let them eat pastry!"

◯ d. "We had joy. We had fun. We had seasons in the sun."

ANSWER KEY

*1, all of the above: People found that Rousseau inspired them to follow their bliss.
2, c, 3, c: But Sophia had big dreams and a bigger brain. 4, a: She did both
quite well, from the sound of things. 5, b: And die well she did.*

CHAPTER SIX

Semimodern Times and More

OUT OF THE MOUTHS OF BABES

I feel old, oh, so old, but I am still the mother of this country, and I suffer its pains as my own child's pains, and I love it in spite of all its sins and horrors. No one can tear a child from its mother's heart and neither can you tear away one's country. . . .

Alexandra Romanov

*S*hock waves from the French Revolution shook Western civilization for generations afterward. Joséphine de Beauharnais, the next royal resident of Marie Antoinette's apartment at the Tuileries, confessed, "I can never be happy here. I can feel the queen's ghost asking me what I am doing in her bed." In 1901, two English lady scholars claimed to have encountered the queen's specter at Versailles; whether or not this was true, they unquestionably had Marie on their minds. Around the same time in Russia, Alexandra Romanov hung in her private quarters a small portrait of the French queen with her children. It offered the empress scant comfort when the Russian Revolution arrived in all its bloody glory in 1917.

Clearly the spirit of egalitarianism was on the rise. As part of this new consciousness, divorce became more widely available, granting women a little more control over their destinies. Divorce also allowed queens to keep their heads after losing their crowns—a pity for poor Anne Boleyn, who was born four centuries too soon.

Just as marital status became fluid, so did the concept of royalty. Blood ties and divine right were replaced by the cult of personality, in which celebrity conferred power. This made it possible for a woman born into poverty to rise to riches and regality. Those who possessed the most influence were famed for their good works or extraordinary beauty and talents. However, the press, instead of the guillotine, gained the ability to make or break a queen. In some ways, the guillotine was kinder.

In this brave new world, royal fatalities arrive in ways that don't require a march to the scaffold: illness, accidents, and the occasional assassin. But the lack of ceremony was often compensated for by burials resonant with mythic overtones.

Eva Perón, the first lady of Argentina, was granted a burial worthy of Cleopatra after she succumbed to uterine cancer in 1952. Her embalmer, who was rumored to have worked on mummifying Lenin, used preserving solutions and wax to transform Evita's earthly remains into an icon worthy of veneration. He even displayed her under glass, like Snow White awaiting her prince. The body of Princess Diana, Evita's populist counterpart in Britain, had no such consecrated public presentation, perhaps because of the car accident that ended her life. Instead, Diana was laid to rest upon a private Avalon-like island, where she still awaits a once-and-future realm forbidden to paparazzi.

Joséphine de Beauharnais

1814

he next female occupant of the French throne bore little resemblance to Marie Antoinette, though she would also end her life crownless. Thirty years before Marie lost her head, the girl who would grow up to become Empress Joséphine was born in Martinique to struggling Creole sugar plantation owners. At the age of ten, Joséphine was told by a fortune teller that she would grow up to marry twice, be widowed once, and become more than a queen—predictions that proved to be all too accurate during a life that often seemed like an overripe romance novel.

Marriage number one was arranged by an aunt in Paris when Joséphine was fifteen. The girl traveled to France to wed Alexandre de Beauharnais, the suave teenage heartthrob of the crumbling French aristocracy. Alexandre was horrified by Joséphine's unpolished island ways. Nonetheless, the wedding proceeded: Alexandre required a bride to claim his inheritance and his mistress was already married. Though they had a son and daughter, their union was unhappy. The couple separated but were reunited in prison during the French Revolution. Alexandre was stripped of his estate and beheaded; Joséphine was condemned five days later. Just as she was about to be marched to the guillotine, she miraculously won a reprieve.

Now free of marital bonds and wealth, Joséphine reinvented herself as a socialite and courtesan par excellence. The Creole sensuality and charm that Alexandre had held in disdain became Joséphine's weapon for survival, seducing numerous well-heeled lovers. It also grabbed the attention of Napoléon Bonaparte, the hail the conquering hero of the French army.

Marriage number two began like something out of a drawing room farce. Joséphine slept with Napoléon, thinking that he would be a useful patron. He pursued her, thinking she had money and social connections to aid his political ambitions. Once the truth was discovered, it was too late: Napoléon was obsessed. Steamy letters record the major-general's pursuit: "How happy I would be if I could assist you at your undressing, the little firm white breast, the adorable face. . . . To live within Josephine is to live in the Elysian fields." He begged her to marry him despite his family's objections—they looked down on Joséphine as a New World tramp.

Immediately after the wedding, Napoléon took off to conquer Italy. Left alone with hostile in-laws, Joséphine comforted herself with an old lover. The Bonapartes made certain the racy gossip reached her husband. "I don't love you anymore," he wrote in a fit of jealousy, "on the contrary, I detest you. You are a vile, mean, beastly slut." Despite these fighting words, Napoléon could not leave her. He also needed her politically—her innate grace and generosity made her Napoléon's greatest diplomat, winning him the devotion of the French people. When he became the emperor of France in 1804, he crowned Joséphine empress, making her more than a queen.

But love was not enough. The emperor required an heir; the empress's sojourn in prison may have left her barren. Five years later, he divorced her—infidelity was tolerable but infertility was not. Joséphine was gracious in defeat: "[H]aving no hope of bearing children who would fulfill the needs of his policies and the interests of France, I am pleased to offer him the greatest proof of attachment and devotion ever offered on this earth."

Within a year, Napoléon married an archduchess of Austria, Marie Louise, who quickly popped out a son. She proved to be as unlucky for him as another Austrian archduchess had been for Louis XVI. By 1814, the emperor had lost his throne and was living in exile on the island of Elba.

As for Joséphine, she retired to preside over a salon that attracted numerous luminaries. Perhaps yearning for her native Martinique, she nurtured a garden famed for its exotic tropical blooms. It indirectly led to her premature death at the age of fifty: While showing off her garden one day, she caught a fatal chill.

CAUTIONARY MORAL
An emperor's loyalty is to his heirs, not his empress.

Caroline of Brunswick

1821

cross the channel in England, Queen Caroline died of an illness that overtook her the evening of the coronation she should have had—but didn't. Her estranged husband, King George IV, made certain of that. He instructed guards to block Caroline's entrance into Westminster Abbey as he was anointed king. Though George had no intention of crowning her as his queen, her presence at the coronation would have granted Caroline a claim he adamantly refused to acknowledge.

Was Caroline poisoned by George's loyalists? No one really knows. But one fact remains certain: George hated Caroline beyond reason. He never would have married her except that he needed money. Plain and simple, Caroline was George's ticket out of bankruptcy.

Caroline's sudden death at the age of fifty-three was just another episode in a bizarre life bejeweled with scandals and eccentricities.

Caroline Amalie Elizabeth was born Duchess of Brunswick, in Germany, in 1768. From an early age, she was noted for her free-and-easy manner—a coarse but friendly informality that would have been appropriate for a fishwife but not for a royal. By the age of twenty-six, when George chose Caroline as his bride,

Caroline on a good day.

149

she had already acquired a reputation for loose morals and vulgar manners. Reservations were swept under the rug for the engagement, since it was all in the family: Caroline's mother, Augusta, was George's father's sister. Though Caroline and George had never met, it didn't matter. First cousins got first dibs at thrones—Caroline was no different.

George was no prize either. The Prince of Wales was thirty-two when he agreed to marry Caroline, and he had already plowed his way through numerous mistresses and spawned illegitimate children. He was obsessed with Maria Fitzherbert, a devout Catholic widow. To win entry to her bed, he secretly wed her. Because his father did not consent to the marriage, lawyers considered it illegal though priests considered it valid. However, George's passion for Mrs. Fitzherbert could not compete with his true loves: gambling, gluttony, drink, and fashion. Such a lifestyle was expensive. The prince's many debts pressed on him, as did the responsibility of siring an heir. If he married, his allowance would be increased and his debts paid.

The first meeting of Caroline and George did not go well. As soon as the princess greeted her future husband, he disentangled himself from her embrace and called for a stiff brandy. He considered her odious and crude; she thought him fat and ugly. The wedding was no better: The Prince of Wales stumbled through it falling-down drunk. Some thought he'd bolt.

Miraculously, the unhappy couple consummated the marriage. Afterward, George vowed "never to touch her again." From this encounter, Caroline became pregnant with their daughter, Charlotte. Fatherhood did not increase the prince's regard for his wife. One day after Charlotte's birth, George revised his will to leave Caroline one shilling. The couple separated.

Much to George's vexation, the public loved Caroline as much as they despised him. Her down-to-earth warmth made her seem one of the people, while the Prince of Wales was judged a dissolute playing dress up in his father's oversize crown; George's father, George III, had lost the colonies and his mind, causing his son to rule in his stead. The prince also won no fans when he refused Caroline access to her daughter, a sordid

Caroline at the height of popularity. George was not amused.

story bandied about by the press. Even Jane Austen wrote a letter in favor of Caroline.

Caroline chose to live abroad, where she indulged in scandal upon scandal. She simply had no sense of propriety, though some were charmed by her openhearted generosity. She took lovers and adopted children as others did kittens, ignoring the gossip generated. Dinner parties often culminated with Caroline dancing seminude for her guests.

Upon the tragic death of Charlotte in childbirth, Caroline lost whatever leverage she had—she was no longer mother to England's future ruler. George took action to divorce her before his father died, so she could never become queen of England. There was one problem: Caroline refused his payout of fifty thousand pounds. She wanted to be the people's queen—a politically dangerous move that could lead to revolution against George's unpopular regime.

When George's father finally died, Caroline returned to England to claim her crown. George decided to force her hand by taking her to trial for adultery, a charge that could result in her execution.

The result was like tossing a lit match to gasoline. Political opportunists jumped

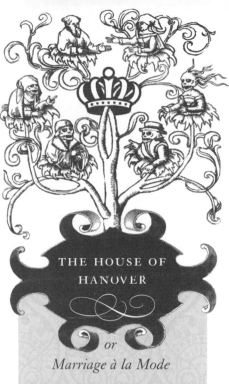

THE HOUSE OF HANOVER

or

Marriage à la Mode

Caroline was asked at her trial if she'd ever committed adultery. She answered yes, but only with the Prince of Wales—he had married her after saying "I do" to a Catholic widow without his father's blessing. So who was George's true wife? You decide.

GEORGE IV
1762—1830

MARIA ANNE
Fitzherbert
married 1785

CAROLINE
of Brunswick
married 1795

CHARLOTTE AUGUSTA
of Wales
1796—1817

King George digesting a good meal. Alone.

onto Caroline's bandwagon, hoping to overthrow the government. The press raged against the crown and reported every sensational detail. Women were especially offended by the king's behavior. Though Caroline emerged victorious, George still refused to acknowledge her as queen of England.

On the night of Caroline's unsuccessful coronation, the uncrowned queen became violently ill with stomach pains. She died less than a month later. Was it poison or illness that killed Caroline? One doctor believed it was a heavy dose of magnesium laced with laudanum Caroline had ingested to help her sleep; it solidified into a deadly obstruction in her bowels. Nonetheless, the convenient timing encouraged rumors of poisoning—all pointed at George. Despite this, George did not contain his joy at her demise. He sang and drank copious quantities of whiskey.

Caroline requested burial in her native Brunswick, far from the king who hated her. Her tomb is simply inscribed, "Caroline of Brunswick, the injured Queen of England." Even in death, she couldn't forget the snub.

CAUTIONARY MORAL
Meet your spouse before you marry him.

LIFE AFTER DEATH

Caroline's story has often been compared to that of another Princess of Wales, Diana Spencer. Like Caroline, Diana found herself in a loveless marriage that became tabloid fodder. The popular princess used her celebrity to influence the press, just as Caroline did. However, Diana was far more savvy at media manipulation. Though Diana avoided poisoning on coronation day, she died tragically nonetheless—but that's another story.

Diana had too much in common with Caroline.

Alute

1875

ying young is a good career move for composers and poets—but not for Chinese empresses. Alute, the consort of the Tongzhi emperor, died at twenty after less than three years occupying the dragon throne of the Qing dynasty. Like her European cohort Caroline of Brunswick, the cause of Alute's premature demise remains unresolved and lends itself to a royal game of Clue. Did the empress succumb to poison in the bedroom? Starvation in the tower? Or, scariest possibility of all, suicide?

Alute's unfortunate fate was unconsciously brought upon by herself—between her exceptional intelligence, beauty, and family position, it was impossible for her to avoid being chosen as empress. Alute was the daughter of Chong Ji, a gifted scholar who served as reader to Tongzhi. A popular story states that Chong kept Alute close to him and oversaw her education. Because of Chong's position at court, the teenage girl was noticed by Tongzhi's mother, the empress dowager Cixi.

Cixi, better known as the Dragon Lady, ruled China as regent for Tongzhi, who became emperor at the age of five. As for Tongzhi, he enjoyed all of the privileges of royalty, but none of the responsibilities. A flop as a monarch,

A most unfortunate empress.

he expended more energy on pursuits of the flesh than his imperial duties. His inexhaustible appetites encompassed male and female prostitutes and transsexuals and possibly left him syphilitic by the age of fifteen. Frustrated at her son's inability to settle down, the empress dowager decided marriage was the cure for her son's worldly woes—and that Alute was the medicine of choice.

Tongzhi went along with his mother's will and married Alute in 1872. Though she was two years older than her husband, she was far less experienced—one cringes to imagine the wedding night between the innocent empress and the sexually voracious emperor. Initially, it seemed like Alute had tamed the beast; he was enthralled by his new wife and insisted on formally accepting the responsibilities of the throne. But within six months, Tongzhi was back making the beast with two backs with everyone outside the palace. A contemporary remarked that the emperor's skill in governing "fell short of even minimal expectation."

Less than three years after their marriage, both were history. Tongzhi suddenly died of what was recorded as smallpox but more likely was complications of syphilis. Alute's death came just seventy-four days after her husband's. She was believed to be pregnant.

No one knows what—or who—caused the empress's death. One theory suggested she was poisoned with gold leaf, a popular mode of murder at the time. The *New York Times* insinuated that her assassination was ordered for political reasons: "[T]here is little attempt to conceal the belief that the fear of complications in case her expected child should be a son led to the sacrifice of her life." Some thought that the empress dowager blamed Alute for her son's fatal illness and took revenge by starving her to death.

But the most logical explanation is also the saddest: Alute was pressured to commit suicide, to win honor by joining her husband in death. It was even rumored that her father smuggled opium to her for the deed.

Whatever may have occurred, the result was the same. Any power Alute might have held was passed back to her mother-in-law, who ruled China with an iron fist for another three decades.

CAUTIONARY MORAL
If your enemies outnumber you, your days may be numbered.

Elisabeth of Bavaria

1898

At the fin de siècle, Vienna quivered with madness. A fascination with the subconscious, as evidenced in the work of Freud and friends, reflected a societal anxiety about what the new century might bring. Elisabeth, Duchess of Bavaria, empress of Austria, and queen of Hungary, was born about twenty years too early to enjoy the full benefits of this zeitgeist. Yet her tortured life reflected the era as accurately as any psychiatric case study—just call Elisabeth a woman ahead of her time.

Though the empress's death would arrive in her sixtieth year at the hands of an anarchist, the sad reality was that her destiny was set by the time she turned fifteen. That was when Elisabeth, better known as Sisi, met Emperor Franz Joseph at a tea in 1852. The emperor, who was a decadent man of the world, fell in love with the innocent teenager, whose wild beauty anticipated that of a circa 1980 Brooke Shields. Franz Joseph proposed marriage soon after; Sisi blushed but accepted. Years later, the empress commented, "Marriage is an absurd arrangement. One is sold as a child at fifteen."

Accepting Franz Joseph as her husband propelled the princess out of her quiet Bavarian childhood into the overwrought world of imperial

Elisabeth in braids.

Syphilis

Any examination of royal fatalities would be incomplete without acknowledging the insidious influence of syphilis, aka the pox. It was estimated that 15 percent of fin de siècle Vienna suffered from it. Upper-crust men were usually infected after sowing their wild oats with prostitutes or actresses. They then carried the disease home to their wives, just as Franz Joseph did to Elisabeth.

After the initial sores healed, syphilis was difficult to diagnose; its symptoms often mimicked other diseases before finally flowering into insanity and death. It was often diagnosed as nervous exhaustion or hypochondria, especially in women, and caused infertility. In Elisabeth's case, it is unclear whether her risk-seeking behavior was a product of disposition or syphilis—perhaps both.

Pre-antibiotics, syphilis was usually treated with mercury supplied in the form of little blue pills or rubs; a popular saying was "one night under Venus, a lifetime under Mercury." Mercury acted as an early form of chemotherapy, slowing the disease by poisoning the victim. Husbands seeking to hide their indiscretions dosed their unsuspecting wives with chocolates laced with mercury.

Vienna. Sisi reacted to the pressure by locking herself in her room, where she wept and refused to eat. When forced to appear in public, the teenaged empress hid her face behind a fan. Soon after her nuptials, she wrote a poem:

> I am awake and I am in my cell.
> I see the chains that bind
> my hands too well.

On the sexual front, the emperor immediately initiated Sisi into the wonders of the flesh, an accomplishment trumpeted to the royal family the morning after the wedding. Four children arrived in 1855, 1856, 1858, and 1868. Another less happy product of their union was syphilis—the emperor had been infected by women of light virtue and brought the joy home to his wife.

As the years passed, Sisi responded to the strain of her situation with increasingly erratic behavior. When her eldest child, Sophie, died of typhoid, Sisi threatened suicide. To gain distance from the royal life she found so oppressive, she rode her horse wildly for hours, risking her neck on dangerous jumps. Sisi's obsession with death extended to a neurotic fear of aging. Her Rapunzel-like hair, which fell like a gossamer veil to her legs, was regularly washed with egg yolks and French cognac. Any hairs that fell out during brushing were counted. To preserve her whip-thin figure, she exercised to the point of collapse and sipped only meat juice.

The emperor's guilt over infecting Sisi left him unable to refuse her anything. He once asked her what she wanted for her birthday; she replied that she wanted a Bengal tiger or a lunatic asylum. It is unknown which gift was ultimately given. As the years passed, Sisi partook of mercury and other therapies to limit her disease's progress. However, the only cure she really responded to was travel. The empress abandoned her royal responsibilities to visit sun-filled locales, swooning over the beauty of nature. To preserve her illusion of freedom, she refused bodyguards and wore heavy veils to disguise her identity.

Family tragedies followed Sisi, despite the miles she put between herself and her life in Vienna. If the empress was to have a soul mate, she found one in her cousin King Ludwig II of Bavaria, whose morbidly romantic nature mirrored her own. Ludwig and Sisi spent hours together riding in idyllic forests, bonding over their shared love of Wagner's music and aesthetics. In 1886, Ludwig was declared insane and drowned under mysterious circumstances. Three years later, Sisi's only son, Rudolf, died with his female lover in what was most likely a suicide pact. For the rest of her life, the empress wore black.

The weight of sorrow and ill health prompted Sisi to ramp up her wanderlust. It was during one of these frenzied pilgrimages that she finally encountered the grim reaper, a suitor she had long courted.

In 1898, Sisi was visiting Lake Geneva with a friend; as usual, she was without protection. A young anarchist approached the empress on the promenade and stabbed her in the heart with a sharpened file. Sisi's corset initially acted as a tourniquet; once it was unlaced to treat the wound, she bled to death. Sisi's last bewildered words were "What has happened?"

A BRIEF DIGRESSION
Luigi Lucheni, the anarchist who murdered Empress Elisabeth, did not have anything against her personally. He admitted, "I struck at the first crowned head that crossed my way. I didn't care." Elisabeth was an easy target—she had few bodyguards because she yearned for freedom of movement. She was also recognizable because she always dressed in black. Lucheni hoped his deed would inspire the masses to revolt against the ruling class. It didn't. Twelve years later, Lucheni hung himself in prison.

CAUTIONARY MORAL
You can't run away from destiny.

157

Alexandra Romanov

1918

nlike Empress Elisabeth, Alexandra Romanov should have had a more fortunate life. Besides possessing enough wealth and beauty to live happily ever after, she was gifted with an unusually loving royal marriage unmarred by venereal disease. But like a fairy tale princess born with a terrible curse, Alexandra bore a legacy that would eventually destroy herself, her family, and an empire.

Alexandra was born in 1872 to Alice, Grand Duchess of Hesse and the daughter of Queen Victoria. As a small child, Alexandra was nicknamed Sunny because of her happy temperament. However, the little German princess was transformed into a somber six-year-old after her mother's sudden death from diphtheria. Cupid made up for this in 1894 when she wed Nicholas II, the tsar of Russia, after a long courtship; though they loved each other madly, Alexandra's religious beliefs made her a reluctant convert to the Russian Orthodox Church. The new tsarina's generous dowry included hemophilia—a curse that became apparent only at the birth of her fifth child and only son, Alexei, heir to the Russian throne.

Though hemophilia occurred as a spontaneous mutation in Queen Victoria's family, inbreeding made the disease rife among the royals. This incurable blood disorder was particularly cruel because it was carried by females, who would remain blissfully unaware of their genetic predilection until a son was born suffering from the disease; most hemophiliacs were male. In those pre–DNA test days, there was no way to know who carried the mutation. Its effects were also unpredictable—a simple bruise could bring on a near-fatal hemorrhage.

Three days after Alexei's birth, what remained of his umbilical cord began to seep blood. This was the first of many near-death episodes for the young tsarevich. His disease transformed the Romanov family into a closely knit unit whose defining modus operandi was to protect Alexei from harm. They surrounded him with a cushy blanket of secrecy—no one wanted the world to know that the next tsar of Russia was a hemophiliac.

It was Alexandra's desperate search for a cure that led her to Rasputin, the Elmer Gantry on steroids of tsarist Russia.

Rasputin has been called the mad monk, a miracle worker, a charlatan, a devil, and a lothario. All of these allegations are true—he was a hornet's nest of contradictions. He styled himself a starets, or spiritual healer of peasant origin, yet he had a superhuman thirst for alcohol and a talent for getting under the ladies' petticoats. He stank like a goat, had pockmarked skin, yet dressed luxuriously. Rasputin's most noted feature was his intense gray eyes, which he used to hypnotize his subjects. Prince Felix Yussupov wrote of a healing session, "I gradually slipped into a drowsy state, as though a powerful narcotic had been administered to me. All I could see was Rasputin's glittering eyes." Many women who came to him for spiritual advice soon found themselves in his putrid embrace; he whispered to them, "You think I am polluting you, but I am not. I am purifying you."

Rasputin arrived in Alexandra's life during Alexei's most severe bleeding episode. Though doctors had written the boy off as worm food, the starets said a few prayers and assured the tsarina that her son would survive. And he did—everyone considered it a miracle. After this, it was a matter of time before Alexandra convinced herself that Alexei would die without Rasputin. The starets soon insinuated himself into every aspect of royal life.

When Russia was forced into war with Germany, Tsar Nicholas was called to the front. Alexandra remained at home with Alexei—and Rasputin. Desperate to help her husband, she consulted the starets for political advice. Government officials were hired and fired willy-nilly, based on whether Rasputin liked them. Unaware of Alexei's disease, people could not comprehend why Rasputin was accorded so much power. Believing the worst, they gossiped that the tsarina had wild orgies with him, that she was using him to destroy Russia. When Alexandra's interference led to governmental chaos, they brought up her German heritage and accused her of spying for the enemy. Pained by these charges, the tsarina protested, "Twenty years have I spent in Russia. . . . All my heart is bound to this country. . . ."

Rasputin's influence could not continue. To save Russia—so they thought—several of the tsar's relatives, one of whom was Prince Yussupov, lured Rasputin to dinner on New Year's Eve, 1916. The starets was as tenacious in death as he was in life. To kill him, the aristocrats poisoned and shot him—still he lived. Finally, they threw Rasputin into the Neva to drown.

Rasputin must have had intimations of his death. He wrote Nicholas several days before his murder, "I feel that I shall leave life before January 1. . . . if it was your relations who have wrought my death then no one in the family, that is to say, none of your children or relations, will remain alive for more than two years. They will be killed by the Russian people."

Rasputin's prediction proved to be all too accurate. Despite the best intentions of Rasputin's assassins, peasants viewed the mad monk's murder as an attack upon one of their own. It inflamed class tensions to revolutionary levels, encouraged by food shortages due to the war and a harsh winter. Hoping to protect his country and family, Nicholas abdicated in 1917. But it mattered little—Alexandra and the rest of her family were imprisoned and executed by firing squad in 1918.

CAUTIONARY MORAL
Don't trust a holy man who acts like the devil.

LIFE AFTER DEATH

The Romanovs' treatment post-assassination makes the denouement of *Fargo* seem a genteel soiree. Their bodies were dismembered, then burned with hundreds of gallons of gasoline and sulfuric acid. What remained was thrown down an abandoned mine shaft, not to be found for another century. However, the church treated the Romanovs far more kindly. It granted Alexandra and her family sainthood—an ironic coda for a woman so reluctant to convert.

An icon depicting the Romanovs in their sainted glory.

Eva Perón

1952

ascist, whore, saint, queen—María Eva Duarte de Perón, the woman better known as Evita, embodied all these roles in her brief life. Though Evita's life would eventually inspire a musical sporting her name, her rise to power bears a greater resemblance to *My Fair Lady*.

Born in 1919, this South American Eliza Doolittle was the bastard daughter of an impoverished seamstress mother. Determined to have a better life, Evita looked to the movies for direction. She ran away at fifteen to Buenos Aires to become an actress and quickly scored some walk-on roles. The secret to Evita's semisuccess was the same as that of other hungry starlets: She slept her way to the middle. This attests to her ambition, since most claim she lacked sex appeal. Years of poverty left Evita sickly and thin; would-be lotharios found themselves nursing her rather than enjoying other bedside activities.

Though Evita flopped on the stage and screen, she hit her stride on the radio where her blatantly plebian accent endeared her to the working class. She soon cleaned up her pronunciation and bleached her hair blond. Evita gained fame in radio plays about female regents such as Marie Antoinette and Catherine the Great. These served as dress rehearsals for her next act, which was jump-started when she met General Juan Perón in 1944; Perón was the charismatic founder of Peronism, a populist movement that infused the ideology of socialism with a soupçon of fascism.

Perón described his first meeting with Evita: "There was a woman of fragile appearance, but with a strong voice, with long blonde hair falling loose to her back and fevered eyes. She said her name was Eva Duarte, that she acted on the radio and that she wanted to help the people. . . ." Perón decided that her radio pedigree was useful for preaching his doctrine to the unwashed masses. He promptly dumped his mistress for Evita, who eagerly espoused all his ideals, fascist or not.

The couple married in 1945; Perón ran for president of Argentina and won. To complete Evita's metamorphosis into a glamorous consort, Perón altered her birth certificate to erase her illegitimacy and destroyed her old films, photographs, and radio recordings. She began wearing couture and subdued her curls into a tight chignon. The transformation was effective: In 1946, *Newsweek* named Evita the "woman behind the throne."

Though she was now first lady, Evita never forgot her humble origins. Just as she had single-mindedly pursued fame, Evita threw herself into her mission to help the poor. To gain political support for Argentina, Perón sent her to Europe in 1947. Yet all Evita could think of was home. Upon her return to Argentina, she launched the Eva Perón Foundation to provide health care, homes, and schools to those lacking basic amenities.

Evita tirelessly embraced her work as if she knew her time was limited—and it was. In 1950, she was diagnosed with uterine cancer at the age of thirty. When her doctor insisted on treatment, she retorted, "I do not want to stay in bed drinking hot toddies. I want to help people today, not tomorrow. And that is how I want to die."

Before she succumbed to the inevitable, Evita was begged to run for vice president of Argentina. She coyly refused, knowing her days were numbered. Nonetheless, the people of Argentina granted Evita the title of Spiritual Leader of the Nation, an honor that accompanied her to the grave in 1952.

CAUTIONARY MORAL
You can't rule from the grave.

Diana Spencer

1997

ow can a woman steal an entire country from a queen? It's easy: Be charismatically photogenic, do good works, and die young in a car crash. It also helps to be divorced from a crown prince and have a gay pop icon sing at your funeral.

To anyone who witnessed the mass hysteria that gripped England after the death of Diana, Princess of Wales, it was clear that her mother-in-law, Elizabeth II, was no longer in charge of the home office. Diana's posthumous coup was the culmination of a process that had begun sixteen years earlier when she, a virginal nursery school teacher of noble blood, tied the knot with Charles, the Prince of Wales, and the most eligible bachelor in the world. Their wedding was televised around the world to almost one billion people. Impressive as this was, Diana's funeral got better ratings.

The couple's marriage was doomed from the start. Diana was raised on a steady diet of Barbara Cartland romances; she was hungry for love to heal the wounds of her parents' nasty divorce. Man-about-town Charles sought a brood mare who wouldn't require too much hand-holding. He had lost his heart some years back to Camilla Shand, but diddled too long to pop the question. After Camilla married another, the prince was left scouring the social registry for a future queen whose knickers were clean of intrigue.

Nineteen-year-old Lady Diana Spencer fit the bill and seemed malleable to boot. She eagerly accepted Charles's proposal with a demure, "Yes, please." Diana was enthralled with Charles, but discovered that Camilla still held sway over him. When she confessed her jealousy, her sister retorted, "Your face is on the tea towels, so it's too late to chicken out now." Things only got worse after the wedding. Charles spent their honeymoon reading Laurens van der Post as Diana paraded in a bikini, swarmed by paparazzi.

I'd like to be a queen in people's hearts but I don't see myself being queen of this country.

Diana

It was soon apparent to all that this new wife of Windsor was not so merry. Perpetually surrounded by press, shy Di did not adjust well to life in a fishbowl where her every move and hairstyle were photographed and dissected on Page Six. She grew dangerously thin from stress-induced bulimia. Nor did Diana win the love she pined for from her husband. Charles resented the wild adoration Diana inspired in his subjects and busied himself anew with Camilla. Still, the princess did not waste time providing the royals with an heir and a spare.

Their marriage limped along for fifteen years, each partner consoling himself or herself with various lovers, scandals, and charity work. Finally, after one of Diana's extramarital phone conversations was illegally recorded and detonated all over the media, she went public with Charles's infidelity in a television interview better suited to *Oprah* than the BBC. The princess told all the world, "There were three of us in this marriage, so it was a bit crowded." Charles met her tit for tat. Also using the telly as his messenger, he confessed he never loved Diana.

The couple's divorce was finalized in 1996. Though Queen Elizabeth relieved Diana of her royal title, her popularity and fame bloomed to absurd heights beyond that of all the other Windsors. To Diana's credit, she used her celebrity to draw attention and money to campaigns against land mines and AIDS. However, her good works did not win her any reprieve from the photographers who relentlessly stalked her around the clock.

One year after her divorce, Diana was killed in a car accident in Paris. She was only thirty-six. She was fleeing the paparazzi and did not use her usual chauffeur; Henri Paul, the replacement, had a blood alcohol level three times over the French legal limit. At her funeral, Diana's brother observed, "[O]f all the ironies about Diana, perhaps the greatest was this— a girl given the name of the ancient goddess of hunting was, in the end, the most hunted person of the modern age."

CAUTIONARY MORAL
Avoid men with cameras and Camillas.

End-of-Chapter Quiz
or
What We Have Learned So Far

1. Which gave the greatest offense to Empress Joséphine's hubby, Napoléon?

○ a. An unwillingness to finance his political aspirations.

○ b. A bed open to extracurricular activities.

○ c. A womb unreceptive to passing on his genes.

○ d. White epaulets after Labor Day.

2. Which of these accomplishments did Caroline of Brunswick *not* achieve, much to her chagrin?

○ a. Getting knocked up after one night of marital congress.

○ b. Having Jane Austen wield her powerful pen on her behalf.

○ c. Winning the hot love of her husband, George IV, along with a coronation.

○ d. Topless dancing—nude, *nude*, NUDE!—on the Continent.

3. Alexandra Romanov believed Rasputin:

○ a. Was a healer with a heart of gold.

○ b. Was a funky-smelling ladies' man.

○ c. Was her best hope for chatting up the peasants.

○ d. Had really nice eyes.

Rasputin is watching you.

4. Which factor led to the death of Elisabeth of Bavaria?

○ a. A wild and crazy family.

○ b. An anarchist with a sharpened file.

○ c. A whomping case of the pox.

○ d. Adolescent poetry.

5. What doomed Diana and Charles's marriage?

○ a. The public preferred the princess to the prince.

○ b. Diana thought Laurens van der Post was a Dutch designer.

○ c. Charles liked the royal tradition of a wife at home, a mistress in the field.

○ d. Diana had read too many Regency romances and mistook Charles's last name for Charming.

CHAPTER FINAL

Are You a Doomed Queen?
A Quiz

OUT OF THE MOUTHS OF BABES

The good, the bad, the hardship, the joy, the tragedy, love, and happiness are all interwoven into one single indescribable whole that is called life. You cannot separate the good from the bad. And, perhaps there is no need to do so either.

Jacqueline Onassis

To become a queen, do you have to rule a country or marry a king? Not necessarily—there are other ways to be considered royal today. For example, take Elizabeth Taylor or Jacqueline Onassis. Would you dare to call either of those grandes dames less than regal? Nowadays, heads of major corporations also bear the all-encompassing powers that rulers of ancient times gained through birthright.

If it's possible to be a queen without royal blood, then it's also possible you may be a doomed queen. Take this quiz to ascertain your royal risk factor. And let the head that wears the crown beware.

SECTION ONE

Choose the answer that most closely reflects your situation.

1. Your main childhood memory is:
○ a. Playing with your friends after school.
○ b. Bucolic summers at the beach house.
○ c. Visits to your rich childless aunt so she would remember you in her will.
○ d. Listening to your family fight, bicker, and haggle.

2. Your education was:
○ a. Public school all the way.
○ b. A good liberal arts education.
○ c. Private school. Then Ivy League with a soupçon of graduate school.
○ d. Why go to school when your family has money? Life is for living, not learning.

3. Your family raised you to:

◯ a. Work hard and live honestly.

◯ b. Have a sense of entitlement.

◯ c. Expect relationships to be fraught with danger.

◯ d. Compete for dominance. Not everyone can be number one.

4. You are attracted to romantic partners who are:

◯ a. Solid and supportive.

◯ b. Sensitive and soulful.

◯ c. Rich and powerful.

◯ d. Self-involved and selfish.

5. What's the best way to meet a husband?

◯ a. Through common interests and friends.

◯ b. Let those close to me set it up. They know what's best for me.

◯ c. Seduce him away from his wife of many years.

◯ d. What husband? I don't want any competition for attention.

6. Your dream vacation is:

◯ a. A family reunion at the old homestead.

◯ b. A relaxing cruise where everything is taken care of.

◯ c. A workshop where you can meet influential people.

◯ d. A bender at the Chateau Marmont, followed by detox at Promises in Malibu.

7. Which of the following film titles best describes your life?

◯ a. *Sense and Sensibility*.

◯ b. *Terms of Endearment*.

◯ c. *Million Dollar Baby*.

◯ d. *Dangerous Liaisons*.

8. Which statement describes your involvement in religion?

◯ a. I believe in the Golden Rule: Do unto others and all that.

◯ b. I will fight with those who don't agree with my beliefs. They're wrong.

◯ c. Cults are fun. All that intensity!

◯ d. I prefer to be the object of worship.

9. At the end of the day, what is most important to you?

○ a. To have a stable but satisfying life. Who cares if it's a little boring?

○ b. To know that I lived each day to its fullest.

○ c. Love, power, glamour, money—it's intoxicating.

○ d. A sense of excitement, even if it means dangerous risks.

SECTION TWO

Answer yes or no.

1. I am married to a powerful man who has had several wives before me.

2. I am married to a powerful man whose previous wives have died under suspicious circumstances.

3. I am married to a powerful man whose previous wives now control major corporations or small countries that serve as tax shelters.

4. I am the single parent of a child.

5. I am the single parent of a child who will inherit money upon reaching legal age.

6. I am the single parent of a child who will inherit a country upon reaching legal age.

7. I am the leader of a country where there is religious unrest.

8. I am the leader of a country where there is political turmoil.

9. I own a large corporation whose shareholders are *very* unhappy.

BONUS QUESTION

Is this statement true for you?

I am related to royalty.

Answer Key

SECTION ONE: *Give yourself 0 points for every a answer you chose; 1 point for every b; 2 points for every c; 3 points for every d.* SECTION TWO: *Give yourself 2 points for every yes answer, 0 for every no.* BONUS QUESTION: *Add 4 points if you have royal blood. Total all your points to learn what your risk factor is for becoming a doomed queen.*

0 to 9 points: While you may not be royally inclined, your humility will gain you many years of life.

10 to 19 points: Blue blood or no, you are more regal than most. Use your powers for good.

20 to 34 points: Mildly in danger of becoming a doomed queen. But the frisson of anxiety makes you attractive to the masses.

35 to 50 points: There's still time to avoid the chopping block. You may live on through infamy, but you're flirting with doom.

AFTERWORD AND SOURCE NOTES

Whatever your score on the preceding quiz, I hope that you found the cautionary tales presented in *Doomed Queens* useful for avoiding an unfortunate end. David McCullough wrote that "history is a guide to navigation in perilous times." If this is true, then too many of the female rulers profiled in this book spent their lives adrift without a compass.

Doomed Queens has been my most research-intensive publication to date. Tragic queens such as Marie Antoinette or Anne Boleyn fill the terrain of many a PBS pledge drive— but what about lesser-known monarchs such as Cleopatra's not so loyal sister Berenice or the teenaged and trapped Blanche of Bourbon? Even with the plump resources of research libraries at my disposal, locating the truth about their reigns often proved to be a tricky proposition. I often felt like Nancy Drew (but minus the blue roadster) as I sought the clues that would reveal the fullness of these queens' sad, but sometimes well-deserved, fates.

Ultimately but not surprisingly, many of these women's lives were buried as footnotes within the histories of kings and wars and dynasties. The writings of ancient historians such as Appian, Dio Cassius, Herodotus, Jordanes, Plutarch, and Tacitus provided me with intriguing and occasionally contradictory insights into the lives of Cleopatra, Olympias, Boudicca, and their contemporaries. Other queens' stories hinged on single sources; nevertheless, I decided to include them, since they were too colorful to ignore. The Bible recounted the saga of bad-to-the-bone Athaliah and her mother, Jezebel. The reign of Anula is recorded in the *Mahavamsa*. The *Han Shu* (or *Book of Han*) offered information about the unnaturally truncated reigns of the Chinese empresses of the Han dynasty.

What follows is a severely edited list of works that I consulted as I worked on *Doomed Queens*; a complete bibliography is posted at www.doomedqueens.com. And remember, those who do not learn from history are doomed to repeat it.

Bell, Rudolph M. *How to Do It: Guides to Good Living for Renaissance Italians*. Chicago: University of Chicago Press, 1999.

Bradford, Ernle. *Cleopatra*. London, New York: Penguin Books, 2000.

Brown, Tina. *The Diana Chronicles*. New York: Doubleday, 2007.

Caillois, Roger. "The Sociology of the Executioner." *The College of Sociology, 1937–39*, edited by Denis Hollier. Minneapolis: University of Minnesota Press, 1988.

Collingridge, Vanessa. *Boudica: The Life and Legends of Britain's Warrior Queen.* Woodstock, NY: Overlook Press, 2006.

Davis-Kimball, Jeannine, with Mona Behan. *Warrior Women: An Archaeologist's Search for History's Hidden Heroines.* New York: Warner Books, 2002.

DeLorme, Eleanor P. *Joséphine: Napoléon's Incomparable Empress.* New York: Harry N. Abrams, 2002.

Denny, Joanna. *Anne Boleyn: A New Life of England's Tragic Queen.* New York: Da Capo Press, 2006.

Fraser, Antonia. *Marie Antoinette: The Journey.* New York: Anchor Books, 2002.

———. *The Warrior Queens.* New York: Vintage Books, 1994.

Frieda, Leonie. *Catherine de Medici: Renaissance Queen of France.* New York: Fourth Estate, 2003.

Garland, Lynda. *Byzantine Empresses: Women and Power in Byzantium, AD 527–1204.* New York: Routledge, 1999.

Green, Peter. *Alexander of Macedon, 356–323 BC: A Historical Biography.* Berkeley: University of California Press, 1991.

Herrin, Judith. *Women in Purple: Rulers of Medieval Byzantium.* Princeton, NJ: Princeton University Press, 2001.

Lindsey, Karen. *Divorced, Beheaded, Survived: A Feminist Reinterpretation of the Wives of Henry VIII.* Reading, MA: Addison-Wesley, 1995.

Massie, Robert K. *Nicholas and Alexandra.* New York: Ballantine Books, 2000.

———. *Peter the Great: His Life and World.* New York: Ballantine Books, 1986.

Parsons, John Carmi, ed. *Medieval Queenship.* New York: St. Martin's Press, 1998.

Perkin, Joan. *Women and Marriage in Nineteenth-Century England.* London: Routledge, 1989.

Perón, Eva. *In My Own Words: Evita.* Translated by Laura Dail. New York: New Press, 1996.

Robins, Jane. *The Trial of Queen Caroline: The Scandalous Affair That Nearly Ended a Monarchy.* New York: Free Press, 2006.

Seagrave, Sterling. *Dragon Lady: The Life and Legend of the Last Empress of China.* New York: Vintage Books, 1993.

Sinclair, Andrew. *Death by Fame: A Life of Elisabeth, Empress of Austria.* New York: St. Martin's Press, 1999.

Starkey, David. *Six Wives: The Queens of Henry VIII.* New York: HarperCollins, 2003.

Tillyard, Stella. *A Royal Affair: George III and His Scandalous Siblings.* New York: Random House, 2006.

Tyldesley, Joyce A. *Chronicle of the Queens of Egypt: From Early Dynastic Times to the Death of Cleopatra.* New York: Thames & Hudson, 2006.

Voltaire. *The Works of Voltaire: A Contemporary Version.* Volume 4. Translated by William F. Fleming. Paris: E. R. DuMont, 1901.

———. *The Works of Voltaire: A Contemporary Version [Ancient and Modern History, V. III France, 1384–Europe, 1599].* Volume 26. Translated by William F. Fleming. Paris: E. R. DuMont, 1901.

Warner, Marina. *The Dragon Empress: Life and Times of Tz'u-hsi, Empress Dowager of China, 1835–1908.* New York: Atheneum, 1986.

Weir, Alison. *The Children of Henry VIII.* New York: Ballantine Books, 1997.

ACKNOWLEDGMENTS

As solitary an undertaking as a book may be, it was impossible to create *Doomed Queens* without help from many sources. It is with grateful mind and heart that I acknowledge all those who so generously helped me as I wrote, designed, and illustrated this book.

I send a big bouquet of thanks to the good people of Broadway Books, most especially my gifted editor, Kristine Puopolo. Kris's incisive wit and wisdom made her a joy to work with. Kris's serenely helpful assistant, Stephanie Bowen, added much to the editorial process. Art director Jean Traina conceptualized and designed *Doomed Queens*' wonderfully Dada-esque cover.

At the Park Literary Group, Theresa Park has been there for me and my books for more than a decade. When I first described what I thought was a very dark and strange book concept, it was Theresa's immediate and warm enthusiasm that convinced me to develop it into what became *Doomed Queens*. For this reason and many others, this book is dedicated to her. Much gratitude also goes out to Shannon O'Keefe, Amanda Cardinale, and Abigail Koons.

The models who gamely posed for the drawings in this book were incredibly patient as I dressed them up in period costume, cheerfully wielding whatever weapon or motivation I threw their way. In alphabetical order, they were: Alice Barrett-Mitchell, Stephanie Bowen, Abraham Danz, Jill Dowling, Monica Hernandez, Lisa Hunt, Annmaria Mazzini, Jo Anna Mitchell, Cassandra O'Neill, Theresa Park, Glen Parker, Jacqueline Parker, Kristine Puopolo, and Diane Saarinen. Also on the art end, the digital resources of the Library of Congress provided many of the historical images peppered throughout this book.

My family and friends were very supportive as I worked on *Doomed Queens*. I am especially grateful to my husband, Thomas Ross Miller, whose scholarship provides me with much inspiration and who always believes in my work. My daughter, Thea, was very tolerant of the long hours I spent working on this book; during this period, Cassandra O'Neill provided us with superb childcare and household support. I am also appreciative of the thoughtful conversation, e-mails, and tireless cheerleading of Ed and Joyce Miller, Jennifer Johnson, Karen Zuegner, Lisa Hunt, my NC posse, Alan Davis, Benjamin Salazar, and Stephanie St. Pierre—thank you all!

INDEX